Mind, Brain and the Path to Happiness

Mind, Brain and the Path to Happiness presents a contemporary account of traditional Buddhist mind training and the pursuit of well-being and happiness in the context of the latest research in psychology and the neuroscience of meditation.

Following the Tibetan Buddhist tradition of Dzogchen, the book guides the reader through the gradual steps in transformation of the practitioner's mind and brain on the path to advanced states of balance, genuine happiness and well-being. Dusana Dorjee explains how the mind training is grounded in philosophical and experiential exploration of the notions of happiness and human potential, and how it refines attention skills and cultivates emotional balance in training of mindfulness, meta-awareness and development of healthy emotions. The book outlines how the practitioner can explore subtle aspects of conscious experience in order to recognize the nature of the mind and reality. At each of the steps on the path, the book provides novel insights into similarities and differences between Buddhist accounts and current psychological and neuroscientific theories and evidence. Throughout the book, the author skillfully combines Buddhist psychology and Western scientific research with examples of meditation practices, highlighting the ultimately practical nature of Buddhist mind training.

Mind, Brain and the Path to Happiness is an important book for health professionals and educators who teach or apply mindfulness and meditation-based techniques in their work, as well as for researchers and students investigating these techniques both in a clinical context and in the emerging field of contemplative science.

Dusana Dorjee, PhD, is a cognitive neuroscientist, lecturer and research lead at the Centre for Mindfulness Research and Practice in the School of Psychology at Bangor University. Her research investigates how meditation, particularly mindfulness, enhances well-being and modifies the mind and brain. Dusana is also a long-term meditation practitioner and teacher in the Tibetan Buddhist tradition of Dzogchen.

Mind, Brain and the Path to Happiness

A guide to Buddhist mind training and the neuroscience of meditation

Dusana Dorjee

Routledge
Taylor & Francis Group

LONDON AND NEW YORK

First published 2014
by Routledge
27 Church Road, Hove, East Sussex BN3 2FA

Simultaneously published in the USA and Canada
by Routledge
711 Third Avenue, New York, NY 10017

Routledge is an imprint of the Taylor & Francis Group, an informa business

British Library Cataloguing in Publication Data
A catalogue record for this book is available from the British Library

Library of Congress Cataloging in Publication Data
Dorjee, Dusana.
 Mind, brain and the path to happiness: a guide to buddhist mind
 training and the neuroscience of meditation/Dusana Dorjee.
  pages cm
  Includes bibliographical references.
 1. Mind and body. 2. Meditation. 3. Buddhism. I. Title.
 BF151.D67 2013
 294.3'4435–dc23   2013009081

ISBN: 978–0–415–62613–2 (hbk)
ISBN: 978–0–415–62614–9 (pbk)
ISBN: 978–1–315–88958–0 (ebk)

Typeset in Times New Roman
by Swales & Willis Ltd, Exeter, Devon

MIX
Paper from
responsible sources
FSC
www.fsc.org   FSC® C004839

Printed and bound in Great Britain by
TJ International Ltd, Padstow, Cornwall

Contents

Preface

This book is the result of my exploration of the mind as a psychologist, neuroscientist, meditation practitioner and teacher. As long as I remember I have been intrigued by questions about the role of our beliefs, perceptions, thoughts – our mind – in health, illness, achievement and coping with challenges. Not surprisingly, my undergraduate and initial postgraduate training was in psychology, particularly its clinical applications. By the end of my studies, however, I ended up with more questions than answers – wondering why we should talk about the mind in terms of cognitive representations, reflexes, personality characteristics or brain function. I started to inquire about the foundations of theories we currently use in diagnosis and therapy of mental illness. So, instead of clinical practice, I decided to pursue doctoral studies in philosophy of mind and science, and later, doctoral training in cognitive science and neuroscience.

In parallel with my academic training in psychology, I began to explore meditation-based techniques in order to enhance my own ability to cope with the demands of everyday life, and its effects on my health. As my personal meditation practice gradually took on more depth and focus, particularly through studies of the Tibetan Buddhist tradition of Dzogchen, I started wondering about scientific evidence on its effects. Initial interest grew into a passion about the potential I could see in the integration of traditional theories and practices of meditation and developments in cognitive science and neuroscience. This transformed my research work as well as my practice and teaching of meditation. My research now focuses on investigation of the effects of meditation-based practices, mostly mindfulness, on the brain and body physiology, especially attention and emotion regulation. In the context of my neuroscientific research, I am particularly interested in the impact of meditation-based mind training on the young population and its potential for enrichment (or balancing) of school curricula. At the same time, I see that traditional Buddhist teachings go beyond the current secular applications of meditation-based practices where they mostly serve as ways to reduce stress and to cope with or prevent illness. I am intrigued by broader implications of meditation training for unlocking our ability to cultivate sustainable happiness, for our personal growth, and development across the lifespan.

I believe that the pioneering potential of meditation-based techniques rests in their ability to integrate aspects of our experience which are central to being human with the rigor of science. To highlight this connection, this book suggests that both from an individual point of view of a person seeking happiness and from the perspective of science the answers to questions about happiness, our potential and life's meaning lie in the exploration and insight into the nature of our mind. Genuine happiness and well-being arise from a balanced mind and can be achieved through mind training targeting motivation, attention, emotion regulation and consciousness. I believe that this new approach to well-being and happiness presents unique opportunities for deepening of our understanding of the mind and brain, their relationship, and their role in illness, health and even the evolution of our society.

Acknowledgments

It was when I started to practice meditation that my passion for scientific research and interest in spirituality began to overlap in my personal and professional life (after running more or less in parallel for about two decades). This would not have happened without the support and encouragement of my teachers, family and friends on both sides of the knowledge continuum. I would particularly like to thank Professor Merrill Garrett, Professor Mike Harnish, Professor Kenneth Forster, and Professor John J.B. Allen for providing me with years of truly enjoyable training in cognitive science and psychophysiology on which I have been building in my research ever since. In addition, I am grateful to Professor Alfred Kaszniak and Professor Guillaume Thierry, who supported and encouraged my interest in meditation research during my doctoral and post-doctoral studies. I would also like to thank my meditation teachers, friends and students who inspired me to write this book. Heartfelt thanks go to my parents for supporting my interest in science from an early age and to my family for their patience and unconditional support during writing of this book. Foremost, I would like to thank Khenchen Lama Rinpoche for embodying and sharing the teachings of Dzogchen.

Introduction

What is happiness? How can we live more happy and satisfying lives? Are there ways to improve our mental balance? Is it possible to enhance the well-being of the whole society? At the personal level, answers to these questions give our lives direction and often determine how we are able to cope with challenges and misfortunes. And perhaps for the first time in modern history, even governments and world leaders are starting to consider well-being of population, not only material wealth, as one of the measures of progress. At the same time, happiness and well-being are becoming increasingly more frequent topics of scientific research and the emerging evidence consistently points to the importance of certain types of mind training in the enhancement of well-being and health. This involves techniques which empower people to improve their mental and physical health from within, through development of stability and resilience of their own minds, rather than through changes in external circumstances. Most widespread examples of such methods include mindfulness-based approaches and programs in cultivation of positive emotions such as compassion. What these methods have in common is the emphasis on the 'power of the mind' and our ability to modify our feelings, thinking patterns, moods and behavior through mental practice.

While presented in the secular context, the vast majority of the currently popular mind training methods cultivating well-being originated in Buddhist meditation practices. For example, elements of Buddhist calm-abiding meditations and inquiry are central to the mindfulness-based stress reduction (MBSR) program, the first and most broadly used mindfulness-based approach. As mindfulness-based techniques and other forms of well-being enhancing mind training are making their way into a variety of contexts in our society – from hospitals to schools and the workplace – it is timely to examine the roots of these practices, the traditional Buddhist ways of mind training for balance.

Buddhist teachings outline an intricate map of the inner world of the human mind with the precision of a scientist. At the same time, they provide practical instructions on how we can transform our minds moment by moment and develop their full potential for balance, compassion and wisdom. This book aims to bring this ancient knowledge into the context of Western science and society by exploring one particular set of Buddhist teachings and practices – those of the Tibetan Buddhist tradition of Dzogchen – in a way which preserves their original completeness and richness in our vastly different cultural environment, yet makes the original teachings relevant and accessible. The goal is to deepen our understanding of mind training for well-being, broaden the scope of its impact and aims, and perhaps inspire further developments in this positive trend.

Science and Buddhism

Neuroscientific studies conducted over the last decade have documented some remarkable positive effects of meditation on the mind and brain. This resulted in an upsurge of interest in meditation-based techniques. However, for practitioners in the West the original Buddhist sources are often quite difficult to access because of their very different historical and cultural contexts. Somewhat surprisingly, it seems that scientific research on meditation grounded in contemplative theory and practice can be helpful in this regard – it can become an effective tool for bringing the meaning of traditional Buddhist teachings closer to the Western audience. In line with this approach, this book presents an overview of topics in Western meditation research in the context of the traditional progression of mind training on the Buddhist path of Dzogchen. In its progression, the book follows the evolution of a practitioner's mind from the perspectives of Dzogchen, Western psychology and neuroscience.

Why Dzogchen? There is a multitude of Buddhist teachings and schools and they all share some core principles and practices. They also differ in some regards – in their particular emphasis on certain forms of practice (ranging from concentration on breath, through debate to visualization), their progression and fruition. Over the last decade, I have closely explored both in theory and practice the Tibetan Buddhist tradition of Dzogchen and related teachings on transitional states of consciousness (such as dreaming and dying). The main feature of Dzogchen teachings and practices is their strong emphasis on experiential examination of the mind by the practitioner. Due to their psychological focus, these cycles of teachings seem to be quite amenable to Western scientific research.

Dzogchen practices have also been attracting increasingly more interest from professionals using meditation-based methods in healthcare and meditation practitioners in the West because of their emphasis on the exploration of the mind.

I believe that the focus on a particular school of Buddhism applied in this book allows for more substantial discussions about the progression of mind training and gradual changes in the mind and brain. The approach here is not comparative – we will not investigate the similarities and differences between Dzogchen and other Buddhist schools. Rather, based on the example of Dzogchen, the aim is to inspire exploration of the progression of mind training in other Buddhist schools and resulting modifications in the mind and brain. Such discussions may highlight similarities and differences in practices which can guide future rigorous research in psychology and neuroscience of meditation. For clarity, in this book the terms 'Buddhism' and 'Buddhist' are used to imply broad applicability across the wide variety of Buddhist schools. Terms such as 'Dzogchen' or other names of Buddhist traditions and schools are mentioned when the field of reference is more specific.

The book aims to provide from a practitioner's perspective an outline of the whole path of the mind's development through the Buddhist mind training in Dzogchen – from the initial confused and unstable state up to the highest levels of balance. While the development of the initial levels of well-being is most relevant to the majority of us, it can be inspiring to explore the more advanced stages of mind training as well. This is also useful with regard to personal progress on the path. Once some level of balance has been achieved, it is easy to confuse mediocre experiences with signs of very advanced balance. The same kind of confusion is some-times visible even in scientific discussions about goals and experiences resulting from meditation-based therapeutic techniques. Familiarity with gradual changes of the mind along the path can perhaps prevent some of these misunderstandings. This is also relevant to evaluation of competence of those who teach meditation-based techniques across religious and secular contexts and may add clarity to descriptions and scientific measures of the effects these techniques have.

The convergence of the inner and outer science

The contemplative path of exploration and refinement of the mind provides a unique opportunity for a meeting of the objective and the subjective, the personal and the scientific. Western science has been built on principles of impartial observation, so that the results of scientific experiments are not influenced by the scientist's feelings, perceptions and thoughts and can be replicated regardless of the observer's state of mind. The human mind, being subject to great individual variability, had therefore been excluded from the realm of scientific exploration for most of scientific history. It has only been over the last two decades that questions about the essence of the human mind and consciousness have made their way into science. Nevertheless, scientists have been applying the same 'outer' approach to its exploration as they would to exploration of cell structures, mostly trying to translate and reduce questions about the mind and consciousness into questions about the brain. This approach is useful, but limited. If we go back to the essential questions about happiness and well-being we started with, scientific answers remain unsatisfactory. Hence, one of the goals of this book is to bring the mind back into the equation, both at the individual and the scientific levels.

The convergence of inner and outer knowledge is very relevant in the broader sense as well, when we go beyond individual well-being. It is becoming more obvious now than ever that progress in our understanding and exploitation of the outside world needs to go hand in hand with the evolution of our mind. Ecological disasters, downturns of financial markets, conflicts and wars are good examples of how unbalanced states of mind fed by anger and greed cause great harm on a large scale. This demonstrates the dangers of separating scientific development focusing on the outside world from the development of our inner world, development of our minds, towards balance, compassion and ethical behavior. In our schools, decades of each person's education are spent in learning about the outside world. But rarely, if ever, do we receive instructions on how to deal with frustration or anxiety and how to develop a healthy mind. This book aims to encourage more curiosity and openness about the balance between inner and outer science. Perhaps we discover that they complement, rather than exclude, each other, or even more, that their balance is necessary for our health, well-being and even the development of our society.

How to work with this book

The book can be read simply to gain better understanding of the progression of Buddhist mind training practices in Dzogchen from psychological and neuroscientific perspectives. However, one of the aims of the book is to highlight the importance of integrating theoretical and experiential understanding of the levels of mind training. Hence each chapter contains simple guided meditations relevant to the level of mind training considered. These meditations do not provide a complete guidance on how to put the theory into practice, but they do present foundational examples of what the relevant meditation practices would involve. This may help readers of various backgrounds to gain better understanding of different kinds of meditation. This combination of theory and practice might be useful to clinicians applying meditation-based approaches in their work since it may elucidate the roots of some of the techniques they use. Such understanding could in turn inspire translation of further meditation methods into clinical practice. It is also my hope that the book will be relevant to students and researchers investigating the effects of meditation since it places individual meditation practices into a broader context of Buddhist mind training and discusses some aspects of meditation practice which have not received a lot of attention in the Western scientific community so far.

Chapter 1

Kinds of happiness

Science and Buddhism: On happiness

We spend our lives searching for happiness. Indeed, both science and Buddhist teachings acknowledge happiness as the main motivating factor of human behavior. However, interpretations of what happiness is differ greatly across traditions and people, as do ways to find it. Many people think that family, relationships and work achievements will make them happy. Others would put money on the top of their happiness list; and some seek happiness in the pursuit of truth or justice. So while we all seek happiness, one of the main tasks in our lives is to understand what happiness is and to choose the right path to find it.

As we start our exploration of kinds of happiness, it can be useful to distinguish two basic types. First, there is hedonistic happiness, bound to pleasure of possessing something desirable. For example, the pleasure of having a fine dinner, driving a new car, looking good, achieving at work, being popular and so on are on the hedonistic scale, all supposed to result in more happiness. If simply judging based on the number of TV programs and events devoted to culinary competitions, popularity contests and fashion shows, hedonistic happiness dominates Western culture. It is, for the most part, the focus of the consumer-oriented society in which various products promise to make us look more attractive, smart or successful. The downside is that hedonistic happiness is usually short-lived and closely bound to its source – if the fine dinner is over, the pleasure which accompanied it is gone as well.

The second type of happiness seeks fulfillment not in pleasure, but in the pursuit of something worthy in the deeper sense. This type of happiness comes from accomplishing our highest potential, from looking for meaning in life, going beyond the ordinary and often reaching beyond our own self. Aristotle used the term eudaimonic happiness to describe this view (Aristotle 1985). In contrast to hedonistic happiness, eudaimonic happiness is longer-lasting. This is because it is linked to our long-term goals, our ways of thinking about life and its meaning, our general mind set or level of awareness. Importantly, eudaimonic happiness is usually not bound to an external source. For the most part, it does not depend on our material possessions and their limitations. So its long-term effects and less reliance on the material make eudaimonic happiness more available and worth pursuing, even though our culture, sadly, does not highlight this enough.

Hedonistic and eudaimonic happiness also differ in their consequences for our well-being. If we focus on hedonistic happiness, we spend our lives constantly seeking new or more potent sources of pleasure. Our minds and brains easily get used to the pleasure-inducing experiences and we want to experience more of them and in a more intensive way. If this craving slips out of control, we can develop an addiction. There are plenty of examples of addictions, ranging from the most obvious kinds such as alcohol and nicotine, to more subtle ones, for instance obsessive shopping. Most of them share similar mechanisms of disruption in brain systems related to motivation, inhibition of behavior and affect (Goodman 2008). For example, some research shows that, at least to some extent, overeating resulting in obesity is linked to an imbalance in pleasure-related neuro-transmitters in the brain (Cota et al. 2006).

In contrast, eudaimonic happiness directly supports our well-being and is much less subject to harmful addictions. It is linked to nourishing experiences which encourage our potential for self-exploration, understanding of the world and our place in it. Reliance on worthy goals develops stability and balance in our lives and helps us overcome challenges and difficulties (Ryff and Singer 2008). In this way, some people are able to turn their struggles with illness, loss and misfortune into a drive to improve the lives of others similarly affected. One example for many: mothers of recently deceased UK soldiers have set up a charity in support of similarly affected families. There are also everyday situations where we can see people developing themselves and contributing to their community: sports coaches helping young people find more grounding in their lives, young people volunteering their time and energy to improve environmental awareness and many more.

When it comes to happiness, Western neuroscience has so far mainly focused on an exploration of pleasure-seeking behavior and avoidance of pain. This research suggests that neurotransmitter changes in frontal lobe structures of the brain, especially the anterior cingulate and orbitofrontal cortex, play a central role in pleasure and pain experiences (Kringelbach and Berridge 2009). The neural basis of eudaimonic happiness is virtually unexplored. It has been proposed, though, that brain structures linked to eudaimonia are mostly different from those involved in hedonistic happiness. They may involve temporal and frontal lobe areas subserving memory and thinking, including contemplations about self.

Buddhist notions of happiness resonate with the concept of eudaimonic happiness and extend it further. The meaning of life from the Dzogchen point of view is in finding the ultimate understanding of our existence and reality. Here the central idea is that genuine happiness cannot be found in the external world, but can only arise from a balanced, compassionate and wise mind. This involves balance of motivation and values, stabilized attention, emotional balance, and finally, a deep understanding of our mind and its place in the world. In this context, compassion and wisdom are the central attributes of a happy and healthy mind and they complement each other. Compassion represents the courage to see our existence, others and the world around us clearly without the preconceptions of stereotypes, fear and avoidance. It increases our ability to see the obvious and also more subtle forms of our and others' suffering, and results in a genuine wish to be free from suffering. This leads to a growing understanding that all forms of suffering originate from a profane and unbalanced mind.

The Buddhist notion of happiness and its development are quite revolutionary. The mind training typically starts with contemplations on the limitations of pleasure-based happiness. In the tradition of Dzogchen the practices show that lasting happiness is to be found in a deeper meaning of life, but what is meant here supersedes usual notions of eudaimonic happiness and includes the ultimate understanding of reality. This wisdom is closely bound to advanced well-being of a healthy balanced mind. Overall, the Buddhist emphasis on mind training provides a unique opportunity for enrichment of psychological and neuroscientific research on happiness. Such collaboration has the potential to transform our knowledge about happiness and well-being, and about ways to develop them fully.

Hedonistic happiness and time

Buddhist teachings point to some fundamental problems of hedonistic happiness, one of them being its impermanence. Pleasure-based happiness is closely bound to its source, and if its source is gone, the pleasure ends. If a relationship makes us happy, we are unhappy when the relationship is over. If we are proud of our achievements, we become unhappy once they are forgotten or when we do not receive the usual praise. In short, change is the ultimate enemy of hedonistic happiness and unfortunately, all sources of pleasure are subject to change. Let's examine this more closely.

Material possessions are the most obvious cases of the impermanent nature of hedonistic happiness. We often crave new things and, when we get them, we feel happy. Buying a new car is a good example. For most people a car purchase is a big event. It often becomes a sign of maturity or a mark of financial independence. In the USA, most teenagers cannot wait until they are 16 and can finally drive their first car. When we get our first job, often one of the first big purchases is a car and there is a lot of initial excitement and pleasure connected to getting it. But a couple of years later, the car we had been so excited about at the beginning shows signs of wear and tear. By now we are well accustomed to using it every day and the initial pleasure is lost. We get mad when the car does not perform reliably and eventually start wishing for a new, better car. This is just one example, but overall, the same cycle from the initial pleasure, through habitual use and then replacement with something new holds for all our material possessions.

From another angle, if we consider the cycle of birth, aging and death, our bodies are subject to the same pattern of change. Throughout life, our bodies create new cells, they serve their purpose and are replaced with new cells. Around the age of 25, our bodies start to show the first signs of aging. Gradually, more wrinkles appear, our cognitive reaction times slow down, our muscles and joints become increasingly worn and around our mid-sixties memory problems become more obvious. Our culture is obsessed with covering up the signs of aging, especially when it comes to appearance. The amount of age-defying cosmetics available is quite overwhelming and some people would literally do whatever it takes to maintain a youthful appearance. But no matter how hard we try, time eventually wins the battle and all of us age and face our inevitable death.

Impermanence takes its toll on our relationships as well. Consider, for example, your childhood friends. You probably do not know where many of them are now and what they are doing; you may have lost contact with most of them. Think about your best friends ten or 20 years ago and your friendships at the moment. Are they the same people? Did some of your former friends move into the category of people you do not have strong feelings for any more? In Buddhism, many teachings comment on the fleeting nature of our relationships, how our friends can become our enemies and our enemies sometimes become our friends. This holds for our romantic relationships as well. Suffice it to say that about 40% of marriages in the West end in divorce (US Census Bureau 2005). To sum up, our relationships are in a constant flux of change.

How about feelings and thoughts? Psychology and neuroscience distinguish between mood and immediate affect (Scherer 1984). Mood is an overarching way we feel for days or weeks whereas affect is the more immediate feeling. Some people are in general more positive than others, but we still have bad days and good days, difficult times when we experience a sad event and times of excitement when something we have hoped for becomes reality. With immediate affect, we often go through many ups and downs in one day or even in one hour. Within a couple of hours we can get good news and then be faced with a problem at work, but have an inspiring evening afterwards. You can try to observe your own experience. How are you feeling right now? How did you feel 20 minutes ago, an hour ago or a couple of hours or days back?

The main point of the foundational teachings of Buddhism is that ordinary pleasurable experiences based on what we have, how we look or feel never last. We can have a nice romantic dinner, but a couple of hours later or the next day the pleasure of the delicate food and pleasant company is lost. Of course, there is nothing wrong with healthy enjoyment of ordinary pleasures. The problem arises when they start to dominate our lives, when they become our main motivation and we do not recognize their fleeting nature. As a result, we develop strong cravings for one thing or another in the belief that they will bring us happiness. In that way we start to act like thirsty people in a desert chasing after the mirage of an oasis which can never quench their thirst. However, it is possible to enjoy the pleasures in the moment without craving and with a clear understanding of their impermanence. Rather than trying to enhance and sustain the pleasures, the sensible approach is to focus our efforts on training our mind in attitudes bringing lasting happiness and contentment without limitations.

The missing element

One of my good friends is a healthy, well-educated middle-class woman, happily married, with two wonderful grown-up children. Just like all of us, she has to deal with life's challenges, but overall, she would be considered quite fortunate by most. From a broader perspective, only a small fraction of a percentage of the world's population has a comparably good material and family situation as she does. Despite all this, my friend is definitely not among the happiest people I have met. Understandably, she is unhappy when faced with a difficulty, but even when everything goes as she wishes, she worries it may all change. So even in the moments of happiness, there is this subtle feeling of loss, as if there was always something missing. She is by far not the only person I know having such an experience. Perhaps most people are going through the same struggle.

Here is an interesting paradox. Most people think that having more money and pleasure will bring them more happiness. But a UNICEF survey shows that children in countries such as the UK and USA report less well-being than children in countries that are materially less developed (UNICEF 2007). Similarly, epidemiological comparisons of depression rates in developed and developing countries point to the same pattern – there is less depression in developing countries. Interpretations of these statistics are complex and many factors, including cultural and religious determinants, may play a role. Nevertheless, the lack of correlation between material wealth and happiness is quite striking here.

So, why is having all the material possessions we need, having friends and family not enough to make us happy? According to Buddhist teachings, the reason is that, regardless of what we have, our mind always oscillates between hope and fear. When we do not have something we desire, we develop a craving for it. Once we have it, we fear that we will lose it. In this way, we can never find contentment and peace. Let's take buying a new computer as a simple example. Maybe the old computer does not perform so well, or we just want to go with the latest trends . . . whatever the reason, we develop this strong wish to get a new computer. We save some money and finally buy the computer. The happiness of having it is often immediately tainted by the worry, sometimes a subtle one, that the new thing may get scratched, stolen, forgotten, broken.

As long as we go from fear to craving and back, again and again, there will always be something missing, no matter what we get or what we achieve. From the perspective of Dzogchen, the missing element is the ability to let go of hope and fear and find a deeper source of contentment that does not change. If we find this space in our mind, we find the genuine lasting happiness that was missing in the impermanent ordinary happiness.

Mind over matter, matter over mind

So how can we train our mind for lasting happiness? Simply put, we can do this through stabilizing our mind, understanding it better and developing highly balanced states of mind. The process of self-exploration we go through as we gradually uncover the ways of our mind can be likened to the cycle of scientific investigation in which one builds hypotheses, tests them and generates new knowledge to build new hypotheses. Instead of a scientific laboratory, our own mind is the laboratory in this case. So, in a way, in the process of mind training for well-being, we become experimenters, building hypotheses about how our mind works, what mental habits make us happy and what mental habits have negative consequences. We build a spiral of knowledge which leads to new hypotheses about our own mind and test these hypotheses on our own experience. Based on this new knowledge we consciously decide how to develop and sustain well-being, joy and happiness in our lives. Nothing is taken for granted; all assumptions and suggestions are put to a strict practical test.

In this process it is useful to consider what well-being is. Well-being usually describes a positive state of health and balance of body and mind. In the West, the emphasis is mainly on the physical aspects of well-being. For example, we know that regular exercise helps to enhance and maintain well-being and negative habits such as smoking and excessive alcohol consumption are destructive to well-being. But in our culture, there is much less focus on harmful mental habits, perhaps because there is limited scientific evidence in this regard. Among the findings that are available, there is a relatively large body of research which links anger and hostility to the development of heart problems (Smith et al. 2004). It has also been shown that increased negative thinking combined with suppression of negative emotions is associated with more risks of heart disease (Pedersen and Denollet 2003). Studies on positive mental habits supporting well-being show a connection between optimism and enhanced well-being (Carvera et al. 2010). However, there is very little scientific evidence on ways to develop positive mental habits.

From the perspective of Dzogchen, mind dominates any notions of health and well-being. When the mind is healthy and balanced, physical health follows naturally. When the body is ill, meditation can be as important in the process of recovery as any material medicine. And even in cases when the body suffers from an incurable illness, the mind can still be healthy and strong. According to this approach, the mind is essential for well-being and any health intervention needs to include a mind training element. Treatment of the body and the effects of medicine aim to support the transformation of the mind. For example, the Tibetan Buddhist tradition contains sets of practices focusing on body yoga, not as a separate form of exercise, but as a way to enhance progress in meditation. Here we can find specific body postures and gentle movement sequences helping to 'heal' negative states of mind such as craving or anger.

Such an approach to well-being can perhaps be likened to the 'mind over matter' view. This is, for the most part, in striking contrast with the

Western biological model of medicine, mainly focusing on chemical and physical ways to influence the body and mind. Undeniably, both the 'mind over matter' and the biological models have their virtues and short-comings. Nevertheless, the prevailing Western approach can be greatly enriched by the discovery, understanding and implementation of some methods of mind training. While the biological model helps to eliminate physical, and to some extent, mental suffering, it ignores the role of the mind; it does not explain or provide the means for achieving well-being and true happiness.

The differences between the Buddhist mind-oriented and Western biological approaches to well-being have deep roots in what we believe exists. The biological model restricts our life, our existence, to the material aspects of our being. If our body ceases to exist, from a scientific reductionist point of view, we cease to exist. But from the Buddhist perspective, there are elements of our mind which do not cease with our body. This has consequences for scientific research on meditation. While the mind and the brain closely interact, there is the possibility that some aspects of mind training may not have distinguishable neural correlates, or may not be measurable using even the most advanced scientific tools currently available. For this reason, from the Buddhist point of view, it may be more accurate to discuss the mind of a Buddha than the Buddha's brain. This issue is often overlooked in current discussions about med-itation and its effects on the brain. It is particularly relevant to research on more advanced stages of mind training and mental balance. Therefore, we will discuss this topic in more detail in chapters focusing on con-sciousness. For now, let's keep in mind this issue as we turn to neuroscientific research on well-being.

Well-being, mind training and neural plasticity

Neural plasticity is a term used to describe modification of our brain through experience. From the moment we are born, our thoughts, actions and feelings leave marks in our brain. The number of connections between brain cells increases ten times during the first year of our life. These connections (dendrites and axons) can be thought of as branches leading a signal from one cell body to another. Until the age of ten, our experience and learning radically shape and modify these cells and their connections. As a result, they become more specialized. For example, some of the neurons and synapses develop sensitivity and efficiency in transmitting information relevant to recognition of shapes in the world or depth vision; others become more attuned to speech or writing. This leads to a substantial trimming down of the original set of neuronal connections so that by the age of ten we end up with about a half of the initial numbers. This apparent loss goes together with more efficiency, specificity and speed in signal transmission, so less does not necessarily mean worse in this case. But with aging, the efficiency of information transmission across brain regions declines and, as a result, for example, our reaction times become slower. Frontal lobes of the brain supporting working memory and solving of complex tasks are especially susceptible to these changes. At a personal level, usually in our sixties, we may notice that our memory is not as precise as it used to be and we are slower to react, solve and respond.

However, the most fascinating aspect of neural plasticity is that no matter how old we are, we can still rewire our brain through mental activity. Contrary to the traditional belief about lack of brain plasticity in adulthood, research conducted over the last two decades strongly supports the opposite view. In fact, learning in adulhood can modify the brain up to the point of noticeable changes in brain volume. Based on what we know at this point, this is particularly the case with regard to the gray matter of the brain which mainly contains brain cell bodies and receptive branches of neurons. For example, a study shows that three months of learning to juggle lead to a significant increase of gray matter thickness in brain areas associated with visual perception and anticipation of objects moving in a complex movement sequence (Draganski et al. 2004). Another study has documented changes in gray matter volume in visual cortex after only two weeks of short daily practice in mirror reading (Ilg et al. 2008). If these activities can result in noticeable changes in brain structure, is it possible, so to speak, to rewire our brain for well-being? Rigorous research conducted over the last decade provides initial insights into the remarkable effects of meditation on brain plasticity. For example, it has been shown that people who practice meditation regularly for years develop thicker gray matter in some parts of the brain, including the frontal cortex. This is particularly interesting if we consider that frontal lobes are the brain regions most affected by aging. Because of this, it has been suggested that meditation practice may slow down the usual progress of brain aging (Lazar et al. 2005). In general, these and similar results show that the practice of meditation, just like some other activities, can have measurable positive effects on the brain.

These findings also refute the mistaken perception held by some that meditation means not doing anything. On the contrary, mind training for well-being involves the development of delicate skills of attentional stability and control, emotion regulation and knowledge about our mind.

For example, it has been shown that meditators can use their attention more efficiently and can notice stimuli people untrained in meditation usually miss (Slagter et al. 2007). More extensive meditation practice also leads to less demand on brain structures involved in sustained attention, and as a result, focusing of attention continuously becomes more effortless (Brefczynski-Lewis et al. 2007). Another study showed that advanced Tibetan Buddhist meditators were able to induce a highly compassionate state of mind at will and this resulted in powerful modulations of their brain wave patterns (Lutz et al. 2004). And mindfulness meditation involving breath awareness has been shown to reduce unhealthy reactions of brain structures associated with anxiety (Goldin and Gross 2010). We will explore these and other findings in detail in the following chapters. At this point it may suffice to say that, based on the research available, the answer to the question whether mind training for well-being can modify our brain for the better is a resounding yes.

Encounters with suffering and death

From an evolutionary point of view, the basic motivation of any species is survival. If we simplify the idea, at an individual level this means that we are striving to avoid suffering and death. This is the dark side of the dichotomy of happiness versus suffering, in which happiness means the absence of suffering and suffering is the opposite of happiness. But moments of suffering and encounters with death are often the most transformative experiences in our lives which can change our life's direction and deepen our understanding of its meaning. They are often moments of crystallization, when all the small unimportant things we have built our lives around fall into the background, and what is really important becomes apparent. This is perhaps why contemplations on impermanence, suffering and death are an essential part of teachings in any of the major world religions.

There are many accounts from people who came close to death because of illness or an accident which emphasize how the survivors' perspective of the world and their role in it changed. They often find that qualities of interconnectedness, genuine happiness and kindness are the most mean-ingful aspects of their lives and start focusing on them more fully. In moments when we are suffering or are witnessing the suffering of others, sources of hedonistic happiness become unimportant. For example, when somebody close to us is in pain, we can find little pleasure in buying new things or worldly achievements. This underscores the fleeting and super-ficial nature of hedonistic happiness.

Attitudes towards death in the West oscillate between strong denial and fascination. On the one hand, we are obsessed with death, at least as long as it does not pertain directly to us. We can take news headlines and movies as good examples. There is hardly a day when a major newspaper or a news website does not include reports on someone's death. And most movies contain at least some element of suffering or death. In fact, in many of them we witness more deaths in an hour than we ever will in real life. On the other hand, our approach to death when it concerns ourselves, or those who are close to us, is mostly characterized by avoidance. We act as if death did not pertain to us or develop unrealistic notions about how we will die. In fact, when college students were asked to envision their own most likely deathbed scenarios, the results were quite unrealistic. An overwhelming majority of students wrote that they would die at home, surrounded by supportive loved ones and would face death in a lucid and alert state of mind (Kastenbaum and Normand 1990). This is in a striking contrast with the statistics. For instance, in the USA approximately 80% of people die in hospitals and nursing homes under heavy medication.

Attitudes towards death in Buddhist cultures are more transparent. Buddhist practitioners remind themselves every day of the impermanent nature of our bodies and contemplate suffering and death. This is because one of the first and most essential teachings of Buddhism concerns the nature of suffering and a way to become free from suffering. In these teachings we first explore different forms of suffering. There are four most obvious forms, summarized in the Buddhist context as birth, old age, sickness and death. There is also a multitude of other kinds of suffering, such as not having enough food or shelter, abuse, etc. But in addition to these, Buddhist teachings emphasize the need to go deeper, to search for more subtle forms of suffering and their roots. This brings us back to the mind, which in the Buddhist tradition contains the seeds of all of our happiness and suffering. The five main mental attitudes resulting in suffering, often referred to as 'poisons' in the Buddhist context, are anger, attachment, jealousy, pride and arrogance. Ignorance is considered the core of all suffering because all other negative emotions such as anger or arrogance and their consequences result from a lack of wisdom.

One of the most essential steps on the path beyond suffering is elimination of the negative mental attitudes and habits related to the mental poisons. In this way, high levels of balance, peace and joy can be achieved. Such highly balanced states are associated with physical health, and in cases when illness is unavoidable, the mental balance is sustained despite disease of the body. Most importantly, elimination of ignorance results in elimination of the extremes of hope and fear, including the fear of death. From the perspective of Dzogchen, understanding of our mind entails the deepest understanding of the process of death and rebirth, and reality as such. Once the essence of our existence is understood, death can be viewed simply as a change in the outer appearance. Ultimate liberation from suffering here means cutting through the compulsory endless cycle of death and rebirth, not having to be born or having to die again, unless one decides to do so on purpose, for the benefit of others.

The question of purpose

In the face of suffering and death, we often end up with many 'whys'. Why do I need to suffer like this? Why me? What is the meaning of all this hardship? At the core of these inquiries is the question of meaning, most centrally, the purpose of our life. Western existentialist tradition developed a philosophy and psychotherapeutic approaches explaining how attribution of meaning determines the direction of our life. One of the most influential psychologists of this approach, Viktor Frankl (2006), claimed that human ability to cope with challenges is primarily determined by the ability to find meaning in the challenge, or more broadly, in life. Frankl, being himself a World War II concentration camp survivor, described many examples of how the ability to find meaning even in the most extreme situations of danger determined people's success in the strife against suffering and death.

Usually not being faced with such extreme circumstances, for many Western people enjoyment of pleasures would be the answer to the question of life's meaning. As fleeting as they may be, it is a common belief that we should maximize and enjoy the hedonistic happiness while we can. From the Buddhist point of view, this is a short-sighted view. The joy coming from a well-trained and balanced mind is not only more stable than any pleasure-based happiness, but also surpasses ordinary happiness in its quality and possibly intensity. Still, while being an inherent part of genuine happiness, the joy itself is not the goal. The final happiness and answer to the question about the meaning of our existence come from truth, from understanding who we are and why we are here. From this perspective, the meaning of life is in finding answers to these hardest questions.

In the Buddhist context, this life is a precious opportunity to progress on our path towards genuine happiness. Mind, being the only aspect of our being moving from one life to another, is what determines our suffering or happiness. Therefore, there is a sense of urgency to use any favorable moment of this life to train our mind for well-being and balance. An important element of this approach is facing the responsibility for our happiness and suffering. If we accept that our happiness mostly depends on the state of our mind and that we are able to change the state of our mind, it is hard to blame someone else if we feel miserable. There can be cases when someone harms us or when our circumstances are very challenging. Such situations are difficult and need to be faced with courage, peace, determination and wisdom. Nevertheless, if we accept that we have the capacity to change how we feel through mind training, we gradually learn to maintain a balanced state of mind despite outer difficulties. Rather than feeling like a boat being tossed around among the waves, we learn skillful ways to direct the boat to a safe place no matter how powerful the storm is.

Taking on the responsibility for how we feel also means developing a strong motivation to engage in training for a more balanced mind. Despite some advertisement claims promoting people or devices which are supposed to bring us peace and happiness in 30 minutes or less, mind training for well-being, just like any other skill, takes time and deter-mination to develop. If we consider how much time we have spent learning to read and write, it is reasonable to expect that mind training for well-being is going to take some time as well. Our mental and physical activity is linked to firing of brain cells.

Those cells that fire together or in close sequence are more likely to fire together again in the future (Hebb 1949). When we learn to write, we train the brain cells coordinating the fine movements of our hand to produce patterns of letters with more and more ease. Similarly, if we have the tendency to get angry easily, the more often we get angry, the more automatic the reaction becomes. On the positive side, if we train our mind to react in a more adaptive way, as difficult as it may be at the beginning, with practice this becomes effortless. And with the right approach, the gradual process of mind transformation can itself become a source of joy, from day to day, from moment to moment. We gradually experience more insights into the nature of our mind, which provides the ultimate answer to the question 'why are we here?' And we may learn that this will answer many other questions about meaning and life we did not consider.

Practice: What is genuine happiness?

Before we start with the first sample practices, it might be useful to distinguish two basic types of meditation. I use the term non-analytical meditation for the first type. Meditations in which we train our attention to stay focused on a specific object while letting go of thinking and analyzing the object would fall into the non-analytical meditation category. Good examples are practices involving focus on breath or some other object, such as a Buddha statue. The second group of practices is called analytical meditations. They rely on focused thinking and aim to deepen our understanding of a topic. For example, we can contemplate the meaning of death or impermanence. Both analytical and non-analytical meditations train our focus and develop more balance. In a non-analytical meditation we monitor and gently direct our attention to the meditative object. When we engage in an analytical meditation, we restrict our thoughts to a certain topic, monitor for any changes in our focus and redirect the flow of thoughts towards the topic of contemplation.

The practices presented in this chapter mainly contain analytical considerations of topics discussed so far and also include initial exercises in non-analytical meditation, particularly breath awareness. You can do the practices sitting on a meditation cushion or simply sitting in a chair. Follow the instructions and spend as little or as much time on the practices as you are comfortable. Now it's time to start the mind training!

Body posture

Our body posture influences our mind. Therefore, it is important to settle the body in a posture that is conducive to mind training. One of the most often-used meditation postures is called seven-point Vairocana posture after the Buddha Vairocana, who is traditionally depicted in paintings in this position.

First, make sure you sit comfortably in a chair or on a cushion. If you are sitting on a cushion in a lotus or half-lotus position with your legs crossed, make sure that your knees are not higher than your hips. Then place your hands one inch below your navel, your right hand resting in the palm of your left hand and the tips of your thumbs touching. If you prefer, simply place your palms on your knees instead.

The most important aspect of your posture is that your spine is as straight as possible. But be careful not to create tension in your body. Straight posture with your chest slightly raised will reduce dullness and sleepiness in your practice. Your abdomen should be slightly pressed against your spine to support the straight posture. For the same reason, the neck should be slightly bent down.

Next, the tip of the tongue should be pressed against the palate behind your front teeth. This reduces saliva production together with the need to swallow. Finally, try to gaze down in the space in front of you about two hand lengths from your nose.

If you find it difficult to remember and follow all these details, just sit straight, comfortably, without tension in your body, but not too relaxed.

Five deep breaths and releasing tension

Now let's start the meditations by centering our body and mind through five deep in-breaths and out-breaths. We will breathe in through the nose deeply into the lower abdomen, hold the breath for a short moment and then breathe out slowly and gently through the mouth. It is important that the out-breath is longer than the in-breath. While breathing in this way, try to focus only on your breath. Notice how the air enters your nostrils, travels down the body and how your lower abdomen expands. Then focus on the breath traveling up and out of your body through your mouth. You can count the breaths. If you feel the need, do the practice longer.

Breathe in, hold your breath and then breathe out, gently and slowly. (Repeat at least five times.)

Contemplations on happiness, impermanence, suffering, and gratefulness

Now we will start with analytical meditations. I will bring up a topic and suggest some thoughts to consider. You can explore how they resonate with your personal experience, what aspect seems more relevant than another. Observe how your views evolve and how this process makes you feel.

Happiness

In this chapter we have discussed two types of happiness: hedonistic happiness and eudaimonic happiness. We have said that hedonistic happiness is short-lived and hard to sustain. Is that true in your experience? Try to think of things that bring you pleasure. Is there the cycle of initial excitement, habituation and then the need for something else? Do you recognize the subtle hope and fear linked to the things and relationships that bring your ordinary happiness? (Spend at least two minutes considering this.)

Now consider eudaimonic happiness that is more lasting. Consider what it would be like to have a happy and balanced mind that is resilient to changes in circumstances. Do you think it is achievable? Do you want to train your mind for more well-being? (Again, spend at least two minutes considering this.)

Impermanence and death

The next topic to consider is impermanence. You can start by contemplating the impermanence of material things. Look around you: are any of the things you can see going be there in 100, 500 or 1000 years? (Approx. two minutes or more.)

Now consider your relationships: examine how they change over time, how people who were your friends ten or 20 years ago are not close to you any more and how those you did not know a couple of years ago are now close to your heart. Examine how our relationships constantly change. (Approx. two minutes or more.)

Now focus on the mental phenomena. Think about how you felt today in the morning and how you felt yesterday in the evening. Was your mood the same? Think about the last hour: did you feel happy, sad, neutral, curious or excited? How did your feelings change and evolve over the hour? (Approx. two minutes or more.)

Finally, let's contemplate our death and dying. Imagine what it will be like to know that you are going to die. What will be important at the time of your death? (Approx. two minutes or more.)

Suffering and its causes

All living beings strive for happiness and try to avoid suffering. In the Buddhist context we usually talk about the suffering of birth, illness, old age and death. Here you can consider all the different types of physical and mental suffering people and other beings are experiencing. (About two minutes or more.)

Now explore how physical and mental types of suffering are interconnected. Is it possible for the mind to remain strong despite physical suffering? Explore the thought that the deepest source of our suffering is our ignorance, not understanding how things really are, not understanding that the ultimate source of genuine happiness comes from a balanced mind filled with compassion and wisdom. (About two minutes or more.)

Now focus on the mind. Let's contemplate the negative emotions of anger, craving, jealousy, pride and ignorance and their consequences. Explore your mental habits. Are there any mental habits that are not good for your well-being? Perhaps you are short-tempered or develop strong cravings? What are the long-term consequences of these habits? Are there any positive mental habits you would like to sustain? (About two minutes or more.)

Gratefulness

Finally, let's recognize the unique opportunities we have to train our minds for well-being every day. You may consider that many people in the world struggle for survival every day and do not have any time for mind training. Appreciate your circumstances, the fact that you can spend at least some time improving yourself and training your mind for happiness. (Two minutes or more.)

You may notice how we spend a lot of time with distractions and unimportant activities and how some of this time could be devoted to mind training for well-being. Resolve to devote at least a small amount of time every day to this and clearly recognize that it is time well spent. Try to use every moment you can to rewire your mind and brain for balance and happiness. (Two minutes or more.)

Summary: Chapter 1

We all build our lives around the search for happiness. Both according to science and according to Buddhism, the quest for happiness is the main drive behind human behavior. However, science and Buddhism differ in their accounts of what is supposed to make us happy. Most research on happiness in Western science, just like Western society, focuses on happiness linked to pleasure – the pleasure of having food and shelter, pleasure of achieving, pleasure of having a good-looking body, pleasure of having material things that make our life easy, pleasure of having a partner, a family. If we have these sources of pleasure, we are happy; if we do not, we are unhappy. However, the sources of pleasure never last, everything in life constantly changes, and so ultimately, pleasure is bound to lose the battle against time. Not recognizing this, we spend our lives in an endless cycle trying to get yet another thing that would bring us happiness.

The Buddhist notion of happiness starts right here, in the recognition of the fleeting nature of pleasure-based happiness. The lasting source of happiness is hidden in our mind and can be unlocked through mental training. This involves cultivation of wholesome motivation, empowerment of the mind through attentional stability, development of emotional well-being and insight into how our mind creates suffering. Current neuroscientific research shows that such training modifies the brain through neuroplasticity in any age. It strengthens the connections in brain regions which are different from those associated with the ups and downs of hedonistic pleasure.

Chapter 2

Intention, human potential and Dzogchen

Science and Buddhism: Two views of human potential

The hierarchy of human motivation

As we have explored in the previous chapter, the search for happiness is for many of us the central force giving our lives direction. At different points in our lives, happiness shapes into different specific goals – for a university student it may be a successful completion of university studies; for somebody starting their first job a wish for independence and economic stability; at some milestones in our career it may be a job promotion; and with maturity also comes the need to find a life partner and perhaps a wish to start a family.

In Western psychology, there are several theories explaining the development of human needs across the lifespan. One of the most widely accepted theories of human motivation was developed by Abraham Maslow (1943). His influential hierarchy of needs has been broadly used in psychology, education, even business and marketing. Maslow describes that at the foundational level of motivation we all strive for basic physiological needs such as food, water and shelter. Once these needs are satisfied we are more concerned about safety, including personal safety, economic stability and family safety. When these basic survival conditions are sufficiently stable, we primarily focus on the needs of belonging and love nurtured in our relationships with friends and loved ones. At the next stage, the needs for achievement and recognition dominate our life. These can range from motivation to receive basic recognition for work and career achievements to striving for fame in the public eye.

If we look at the situation in developed countries, most of us do not need to be concerned with very basic survival needs. Despite great differences in personal material wealth, the majority of our population has enough to eat, a place to live and the very basic needs of safety are covered. As a result, the focus on needs of belonging is quite central in our lives – whether we look at teenagers striving to fit into their peer group or adults looking for a life partner. But perhaps even more so, the needs for achievement and recognition dominate our culture – our education focuses on academic achievement; our culture cherishes stories of success, be they in business, science, sports or art. Reality shows continuously deliver messages of quick success which in many, particularly young, minds are equated with happiness. Under the influence of media and business marketing, the notion of happiness is presented as synonymous with material wealth, popularity and beauty. There is little room for eudaimonic happiness in the popularity contest world of TV and the internet.

Going back to Maslow's hierarchy of needs, achievement and success are actually not at the very top of human aspirations. The final level of motivation is less dependent on others' opinions, popular views and cultural pressures than the need for achievement. It encompasses self-actualization, satisfaction arising from accomplishing one's potential in terms of talent, abilities and skills. At this level, Maslow uses self-actualization examples of artists and innovators finding fulfillment in their work. Equally so, the self-actualization experience can for others arise from being able to care for their family, or from engagement in their hobbies. Self-actualization means understanding and engaging in what we enjoy doing without expectation for recognition from others; it means gaining deep satisfaction from these activities themselves.

While the motivation needs at different levels of Maslow's hierarchy can be intertwined and more than one level of needs can dominate our life at each point in time, the progression from one level to another is more or less gradual. In other words, according to Maslow it would be difficult to proceed to needs of self-actualization if the more basic needs of safety or survival are not satisfied. Interestingly, though, if we look more closely, all the levels actually share the same focus. They are all about the 'I' and 'mine' – about 'my' hunger and 'my' house, 'my' family's safety, 'my' partner and friends, 'my' achievements and 'my' self-actualization. They arise from the self-centered perspective of who we are and what we need.

Importantly, in his later writings, Maslow added another level of motivation which represents the pinnacle of human potential (Koltko-Rivera 2006). This level goes beyond the individual selfhood, the self-centered perspective. It arises when a person is motivated by and finds satisfaction in striving and experiences beyond the self-gratification of self-actualization. These experiences supersede the self-focus – good examples are the self-transcending experiences of justice, truth, beauty. For some, walks in nature accompanied by experiences of unity with the surroundings which override ordinary ways of thinking evoke these perceptions, feelings and emotions. For others, it would be a sense of connection with deeper truth which sometimes paradoxically arises when we are faced with challenging life events, such as the death of a loved one. These experiences are often described as oneness with an existential element which transcends the differences between the self and the other. They can encompass service to others and feelings of something greater than self, greater humanity and unity of human experience. To capture the specific 'mind mode' of these experiences Maslow uses the term being cognition – a type of awareness or cognitive functioning which is experiential, based on a complex mix of feelings, perceptions and affect in the current moment, rather than reasoning, logical analysis or evaluation. It includes an element of non-judgment, self-expansion, common humanity, warmth and compassion. It puts personal goals and individual achievements into the background of the mind.

The will to meaning

While for Maslow self-transcendence presents the highest level of human motivation, for other psychologists, such as Viktor Frankl, self-transcendence is a much more fundamental force, even the primary drive of human behavior. Rather than focusing on self-transcending experiences, Frankl described self-transcendence as the 'will to meaning', the drive to 'find and fulfil meaning and purpose' in life (Frankl 1966: 98). Frankl considers self-transcendence to be the essence of our existence (p. 104), which means reaching for ideals or values such as greater good, God or universal conscience. From this perspective, focus on self-actualization of one's talents and skills developed without the self-transcending element can even be viewed as a failure to accomplish the fulfillment of meaning or purpose in life. According to Frankl, the will for meaning is the central force in human life, and hence, mental balance and health of a person are closely linked to fulfillment of life's purpose. The inability to recognize and strive for meaning or purpose in life can result in existential crisis, meaninglessness, and apathy which manifest in mental illness such as depression.

Recognizing the essential role of self-transcendence, several recent research studies tried to capture the human tendency towards self-transcendence. According to some researchers (most notably Robert

Cloninger), self-transcendence is an important aspect of personality which markedly shapes our tendencies, thoughts, feelings and behavior. In order to measure the effects of self-transcendence, Cloninger and his colleagues (1994) developed a questionnaire (Temperament and Character Inventory (TCI)) which includes self-transcendence as one of its dimensions. Research using TCI shows that self-transcendence serves as a mediator in the development of positive psychological dimensions such as optimism and emotional well-being in challenging life situations, for example when one is faced with a life-changing diagnosis such as cancer (Matthews and Cook 2009).

Increasingly more studies are also addressing questions about links between self-transcendence and brain functioning. Most notably, research extending psychological research using TCI into neuroscience linked self-transcendence to functioning of a network of brain regions spreading across frontal, temporal and parietal areas. Some studies suggest that parietal areas are particularly relevant to the spiritual experiences of self-transcendence (Urgesi et al. 2010). What conclusions we draw from such research on brain and self-transcendence will depend on our beliefs about the relationship between mind and brain. For some, pointing to brain regions linked to self-transcendence explains the self-transcending experience fully. For others, it adds an interesting piece to the puzzle linking mind and brain, but does not necessarily explain what self-transcendence is. We will return to these and similar questions about the relationship between mind, brain and body in Chapter 6. Let's now explore how Buddhist approaches to human potential map on to notions of self-actualization and self-transcendence.

Buddhism on human potential

Buddhist views of human potential focus on the self-transcending element of motivation, but conceptualize it differently from Western psychologists and also take it further. As an example, we can consider the first set of teachings delivered more than 2,500 years ago by Buddha Shakyamuni after he reached enlightenment. These teachings are summarized as 'the four noble truths' (Gethin 1998) and explain that the central motivation of all beings is the wish to be free from suffering (Pāli: dukkha; Sanskrit: duḥkha; Tibetan: sdug bsngal). Suffering in Buddhism is a very broad term which includes obvious physical and mental hardship such as illness, abuse and lack of essential needs, but also includes more subtle experiences, for instance general notions of not being content, dissatisfaction and anxiety in its multiple forms. Buddha invites his students to examine different forms of suffering and their causes based on their personal life experience. He suggests that the deep roots of suffering are not found in the external world but in the mind. He also describes a way to reach freedom from suffering which involves understanding how our mind works – how the mind gives rise to our experience of suffering and how it is at the same time the key to cessation of suffering.

Buddha's approach is highly empirical and experimental, based on learning from our own experience by careful examination of our mind. He emphasizes that none of his teachings are to be accepted without being put to strict tests against personal experience. Buddha says that, just like a goldsmith in a market examines carefully every piece of gold he is offered, in the same way, all students listening to his teachings should put these to a rigorous test against their life experience. According to Buddha, the experiential study of our own life, behavior and mind culminates in the deep understanding that the notion of our own 'self' is not permanent or true in any solid sense. We build notions of who we are, notions of our 'self' based on our personal history, what others tell us about ourselves, labels our society puts on us. In this way we identify ourselves as confident or anxious, successful or not, citizens, students, members, artists, teachers, administrators, parents, and so on. While these labels have their roles in our lives, clinging to these notions of self and identi-fying with them too narrowly becomes a source of our suffering. From the perspective of Dzogchen, in such a narrow-minded state of perception and thinking we do not recognize that there is an element of our mind beyond the ordinary 'I', 'me', 'mine', which surpasses labels, the self, suffering and its causes. The highest human potential is in recognizing, connecting with and stabilizing the mind in this pure element of con-sciousness.

It may seem that the Buddhist notion of human potential is similar to Frankl's drive for purpose and meaning in life. Indeed, there may be some similarities in the self-transcending connection to something greater than an individual. However, the Buddhist approach is empirical, rather than analytical, and does not rely on idols. Buddhism does not contain a notion of a God, a supreme being or an abstract absolute (Wallace 2007). In Buddhism the emphasis is on our own experience, the first-person exploration of our mind and its role in our suffering and happiness. Critical thinking has its place in such examination, but the further we go on the path of self-exploration, the more we rely on novel modes of knowledge based on phenomenological 'what it feels like' aspects of our experience. This may bear some similarities to the being mode of cognition described by Maslow, yet seems to be a more complete map of knowledge and experience about our mind than a set of self-transcending experiences. Buddhist approaches to mind training result in a radical remake of our mind and aim to stabilize the mind in the mode of highest potential which is free from suffering in all its forms. Here the notion of freedom from suffering is not naïve; it does not mean that we never get sick or encounter situations which would be perceived as frustrating or harmful at the ordinary levels. The freedom from suffering comes from a deep understanding of how our mind creates the experiences of illness, frustration and harm, and the ability to liberate the roots of their experiential arising.

The unique aspect of the Buddhist approach to human potential is that it not only describes human motivation and needs but also outlines a clear path of mind training which leads to accomplishment of the highest potential. Psychotherapeutic techniques based on Maslow's hierarchy of needs or Frankl's notions of self-transcendence have made valuable contributions in the Western psychological context, and perhaps to some extent also paved the way for mindfulness-based approaches inspired by Buddhist teachings. At the same time it can be useful to recognize that Western notions of human potential do not encompass the richness and completeness of the Buddhist approach which outlines a progression of mental practices designed to support the mind in accomplishing its highest potential.

Buddhist traditions and the path of Dzogchen

The path to freedom from suffering takes on different forms across Buddhist schools. Buddhist traditions are often described in three main groups: Theravāda (predominant in Southeast Asia), Mahāyāna (China, Vietnam and Japan) and Vajrayāna (Tibetan Buddhism) (Powers 1995; Mitchell 2002). Each of these three main Buddhist approaches further divides into numerous schools and lineages. According to Tibetan Buddhist scholars, Buddha Shakyamuni provided teachings in each of the three main traditions and these were recorded and further elaborated by other Buddhist masters. Buddha's teachings are often summarized as 84,000 ways to gain freedom from suffering. The variety of teachings is aimed to match the numerous needs, skills and capacities of beings.

Just as there are core similarities between the different Buddhist traditions and approaches, there are also differences in their focus. In Theravāda, while recognizing the interconnected nature of human existence, the primary focus is on self-liberation. In Mahāyāna, the emphasis is on liberation of oneself and all sentient beings. This follows the attitude of the Boddhisattva – a being who vows to work tirelessly to free all beings from suffering after reaching her own liberation. The same spirit of far-reaching compassion is embraced in Tibetan Buddhism (Vajrayāna) with an added urgency to liberate oneself and all beings from suffering as soon as possible. This is reflected in practices aimed to speed up progress on the spiritual path.

While all three traditions share the same aim – achievement of freedom from suffering – according to Tibetan Buddhist sources their actual fruition is somewhat different (Powers 1995). At its core, freedom from suffering comes when one overcomes the fundamental sources of suffering in the mind – craving, anger and ignorance. This is achieved by a combination of practices which settle the mind to the point when its habits become more apparent, contemplation and examination of conducive and harmful processes of the mind, examination of the nature of our self, etc. Critical analysis has its solid place in this process, but the mind also gradually moves towards a new mode of knowing, one which taps into experiential 'feeling' and 'perceiving' of the varied flavours of awareness. As the processes of the mind become more apparent, the understanding of the roots of suffering grows, as do skills of the mind to move beyond suffering. When the practitioner stabilizes the mind in the state free from the sources of suffering, the goal of the path has been reached. This is the fruition in the Theravāda teachings. From the perspective of the Mahāyāna schools, fruition of the Mahāyāna approach adds to the freedom from suffering another layer of knowledge which enables the realized practitioner to guide sentient beings to the same result. Vajrayāna path achieves the fruition of Theravāda and Mahāyāna and aims to do so in less time. There are also additional signs of accomplishment manifesting for Vajrayāna practitioners, mostly at the time of death. These differences in fruition present the views of Mahāyāna and Vajrayāna schools and are not necessarily shared by scholars and practitioners of Theravāda (Powers 1995). Nevertheless, these outlined distinctions are relevant to our discussions about the most advanced stages of accomplishment in Dzogchen (Chapter 5) which are considered the highest fruition of Vajrayāna and differ from descriptions of accomplished states in Theravāda.

Dzogchen

Dzogchen is a tradition of Tibetan Buddhism which focuses on direct understanding of the innate pristine nature of awareness. Within the system of Tibetan Buddhism, Dzogchen is classified as the highest of the teachings (Ati-yoga) (Dalai Lama 2000). It is often described as a group of teachings and practices focusing on non-duality because of their focus on dissolution of the dualistic perception of us as the observer and the other as the observed. An experiential example might be useful here. If you look at the things around you in this very moment, you probably see in front of you a book you are reading and there is a sense of you (maybe your mind) observing the book out there. You are, or your mind is, the subject, 'the observer', and the book is the object in the process of observation, 'the observed'. The tradition of Dzogchen recognizes that this duality of perception is at the core of our suffering and experiential breaking through this duality is the key to understanding the reality of our own self and the reality around us. The realization of non-duality and revelation of the inner and outer reality as such are distinctive to Dzogchen. Theravāda emphasizes the notion of a construed self developed through our thoughts and stereotypes, but does not consider the dualistic reality of the self and the outside world. And in Mahāyāna the concept of the non-duality is mostly marginal, even though it is a matter of debate whether some Mahāyāna teachings, such as Mahamudra, contain non-dual teachings similar to Dzogchen.

The origins of Dzogchen are traced back to the time before Buddhist teachings made their way to Tibet from India. Within the Tibetan Buddhist tradition, Dzogchen is most prominently represented within the Nyingma lineage (the old school) starting with the founder of Tibetan Buddhism, Padmasambhava (8th century). Aside from Padmasambhava, the main teachings of Dzogchen in Tibet were authored by Longchen Rabjam (14th century; Rabjam 1998, 2010), Jigmed Lingpa (18th century), Patrul Rinpoche (19th century; Patrul Rinpoche 1998) and Mipham Rinpoche (19th to 20th century; Mipham Rinpoche 1997). The most well-known recent masters of Dzogchen were H.H. Jigmed Phuntsok Rinpoche and Dilgo Khyentse Rinpoche. This book builds on teachings by all these teachers.

Because of its explicit focus on mind training and exploration of the mind, Dzogchen is particularly amenable to bridging Buddhist teachings with Western psychology, cognitive science and neuroscience. Dzogchen teachings provide a clear outline of the evolution of a practitioner's mind from the initial unstable state to the highest levels of insight (Logchen Rabjam, *The Seven Treasuries*; Jigmed Lingpa, *The Treasury of Enlightened Attributes*). Understanding of these stages is of utmost relevance to current research in psychology and neuroscience of meditation which, partially because of the nascent nature of the field, is often marked by a lack of distinctions between outcomes of foundational and advanced practices. For example, the notion of 'direct perception' is commonly used to describe preliminary experiences arising from secular mindfulness practice (Brown et al. 2007), but in Dzogchen direct perception designates profound states of realizing non-duality (Rosch 2007; Dorjee 2010). Better understanding of stages of Buddhist mind training can also help clarify some theoretical issues, for example, the differences between focused and open meditation (Lutz et al. 2008a), since what is considered to fall under these labels varies greatly with depth of practice and its outcomes. The terms focused and open meditation are currently being used across secular and Buddhist meditation traditions in reference to states which are arguably qualitatively different and reflect different stages of contemplative training (Dzogchen: Lutz et al. 2007; Vipassana: Slagter et al. 2007; and mindfulness: Jha et al. 2007). A contextualized approach to contemplative psychology and neuroscience can lead to the formulation of more precise hypotheses about the effects of meditation on the mind and brain.

The gradual transformation of the practitioner's mind through contemplative mind training is in the Dzogchen writings described from the first-person experiential perspective of the practitioner – from the practitioner's observation, reflection and exploration of the processes of her own mind. This is complemented by expert accounts of Dzogchen masters whose minds have been refined to detect subtle signs of students' progress. The refinement of the practitioner's mind is often summarized in Dzogchen teachings in terms of 13 or 16 levels of progression (Logchen Rabjam, *The Seven Treasuries*; Jigmed Lingpa, *The Treasury of Enlightened Attributes*), but can be briefly described in three basic stages.

The foundational level of training in Dzogchen builds basic stability of the mind through the development of virtuous motivation for the practice and through calm-abiding practices which refine the attention in order to make it a suitable tool for observation of the processes of the mind. This foundational training involves practices based on analytical thinking such as contemplations about what brings us happiness and what results in suffering, as well as practices training the ability of the mind to let go of negative thought patterns. The second stage of training in Dzogchen includes deepening of the basic levels of concentration and initial experiential investigation of the nature of the mind. In this process, students typically work more closely with an accomplished teacher who 'points out' the non-dualistic nature of the mind to them and this powerful experience bootstraps students' progress on the path. Even though students gradually become more able to distinguish experientially the ordinary fleeting experiences of the mind from the more subtle ones which are closer to the nature of the mind, their realization is still unstable and can be rather shallow. The third stage represents the fruition of the practitioner's training in Dzogchen. The experiential understanding of the nature of the mind takes on increasingly more depth and the dualistic perception of the subject and object experientially dissolves. This realization gradually approaches the level of understanding described as enlightenment. In terms of psychological attributes developed and modified on the path, Dzogchen teachings describe gradual development of generosity, ethical discernment, patience, concentration, and different levels of wisdom and insight.

Complexity of meditation research and the pyramid of mind training in Dzogchen

With the increasing popularity of scientific reports on how meditation modifies the mind and brain, it is important to acknowledge that this type of research faces many complexities not typical of other psychological or neuroscientific studies. First, the difficulty arises from the great variety of meditation practices and meditation approaches. On top of that, even practices with the same name – such as mindfulness – can differ greatly across meditation schools (Dorjee 2010). In addition, each meditation practice is usually not a standalone; rather, it is a piece in the puzzle of a larger system of mind training and philosophical attitudes. This is particularly the case within Buddhist traditions, but also holds for many secular forms of meditation. For example, a mindfulness-based stress reduction program involves not only training in mindfulness as such but also education about stress, sharing of experience in a group setting, elements of contemplative inquiry, yoga, and chi-gong exercises. So is it really possible to single out one meditation practice or another in research and measure its effects on the mind and brain under the assumption that the practice itself is solely responsible for these effects without the contribution of the whole system of beliefs and mind training methods in which the practice was acquired?

In response to this complexity, it can be useful to combine 'microscopic' and large-scale views of each meditation practice in research. While the microscopic view focuses on nuances of a particular practice, the large-scale approach enables us to zoom out to the level of the whole system of meditation training in which the practice originated and look at the place of the specific practice in it. For example, if we were to explore the effects of a compassion meditation practice within the Tibetan

Buddhist tradition, we might first look at the particular form of the practice, how it aims to develop the quality of compassion and differs from compassion practices in other Buddhist traditions and schools. We may for instance ask whether the practice involves visualization or contemplative inquiry, or both. We may examine the inclusiveness of the compassion practice, whether it progresses from compassion for an individual to a broad view encompassing all beings or even non-conceptual compassion. In the second step of the investigation we may want to take an airplane view of the practices in the particular Tibetan Buddhist tradition we are exploring and see where the compassion practice fits in the whole scheme of mind training. We may explore whether this particular compassion practice is taken on after proficiency has been achieved in other meditation practices such as mindfulness; whether the compassion meditation is a prerequisite for other practices; and whether there are different levels of depth in the compassion practice. By applying this comparative approach, we can build hypotheses about minute differences in activation and function of systems in the mind and brain which underlie the practice. For instance, it is likely that compassion meditation involving visualization practice requires more activation in the visuospatial systems of working memory (Kozhevnikov et al. 2009), whereas analytical meditation involving thinking about different kinds of compassion will lead to activation of areas of the brain associated with speech (even if it is silent speech linked to thinking). In addition, the activation of these systems may be different in a practitioner who trained in mindfulness first and perhaps gained more attentional stability to start with. In contrast, a distinct pattern of activation may be found in a practitioner who first engaged in foundational practices such as contemplations on the four noble truths which enhanced the strength of her motivation to engage in the training of compassion and gave it more depth.

Four aspects of well-being

In order to capture this richness of meditation training, we may need to apply a more complete systemic approach when considering modifications in mind and brain resulting from meditation practice. Alan Wallace and Shauna Shapiro (2006) provided a foundation for such an approach when they linked Buddhist mind training to changes in four aspects of psychological well-being: conative, attentional, cognitive and affective. The conative element of well-being relates to the intention with which the practitioner engages in meditation practice, with more balance arising when we focus on eudaimonic happiness for ourself and others.

Attentional balance is about the stability of our attention and the ability to observe the mind with clarity. The cognitive aspect of well-being describes balance of thinking patterns where excessive repetitive thinking on one hand and apathy on the other side of the continuum are the most obvious disturbances of the equilibrium. Finally, affective balance pertains to emotional well-being.

These four aspects of well-being can serve as points of reference when considering the effects of a meditation practice on well-being, with some practices and disorders working with one of the aspects more so than others. For example, Wallace and Shapiro (2006) discuss cases of conative dysfunction such as addictions, and at a more subtle level, disturbances of motivation when someone is driven by superficial goals of fame or financial success. They also consider practices intended to cultivate conative balance involving reflection on desires and goals in life, and their consequences. These practices are foundational in the Tibetan Buddhist tradition and their aim is to highlight to the practitioner, based on the examination of their own experience, which goals in their life lead to well-being and which are detrimental to it.

The pyramid of mind training in Dzogchen

Building on the conception of well-being suggested by Wallace and Shapiro (2006) and extending it further, we can bridge the traditional steps of mind training in Dzogchen with a theory about corresponding changes in systems of mind and brain. In this new conception we will map the traditional progression of the mind's evolution in Dzogchen as a gradual rewiring of the mind and brain at four basic levels, represented as a pyramid of mind training. Similarly to Wallace and Shapiro (2006), the first two levels are about the intention for the mind training and the abilities of the mind to focus and guide attention. This similarity is not surprising, since the progression of foundational levels of mind training is shared across Buddhist approaches, even though the practices used to train the mind may differ. However, the next two steps in the pyramid of mind training are more specific to the Dzogchen tradition and therefore depart to some extent from the cognitive and emotional aspects of well-being proposed by Wallace and Shapiro (2006). The third level aims to develop emotional balance and also encompasses many elements of training in cognitive balance. At the final level, the stable, focused and fairly balanced mind becomes a tool for exploration of the different notions of 'self' and the deepest self-transcending element of consciousness. Let's review the four levels more closely.

For any traditional Buddhist form of mind training, the first level – developing wholesome motivation for meditation – presents the foundation for any further practice. The mind training would typically start with a sobering review of the adept's life and an initial recognition of what attitudes, behaviors and actions bring us contentment. This level reflects the key aspects of Buddhist philosophy, examining the nature of suffering and freedom from suffering. We have considered different kinds of happiness in the first chapter to highlight this level of mind training and suggested that lasting happiness comes from a balanced mind which can be cultivated through mind training. In this chapter we are extending this discussion by looking more closely at the views of human potential and intention in Western psychology and Dzogchen. From the neuroscientific perspective we do not know what brain systems underlie complex processes associated with motivation guiding a practitioner's meditation, but related research suggests the involvement of several brain areas in the frontal cortex. For example, hedonistic happiness has been linked to activation in the anterior cingulate and orbitofrontal cortex whereas eudaimonic happiness, which involves long-term goals and self-reflection, may be more closely associated with medial-prefrontal cortex and posterior cingulate (Johnson et al. 2002).

The second level of the pyramid of mind training in Dzogchen focuses on stabilization and refinement of attention. When we start to investigate the inner life of our mind more closely, automatic and often negative mental habits become more obvious. The task is to loosen up these automatic reactions and gently redirect the mind towards well-being-enhancing mental activity. In support of this traditional approach, current research on changes in attention induced by meditation training shows that meditation improves efficiency of attention (Slagter et al. 2007) and the ability to sustain attention for longer (MacLean et al. 2010). With regard to brain regions most likely involved, sustained and selective attention has been associated with frontoparietal networks (Corbetta and Shulman 2002) and activation of dorsolateral prefrontal cortex with monitoring of attention (Ridderinkhof et al. 2004).

The third level of training in Dzogchen entails a radical emotional remake of the practitioner's mind. One learns techniques which reduce the automatic engagement in negative emotions and cultivate wholesome emotions instead. Deep experiential understanding of different aspects of empathy, compassion and other wholesome emotions plays a central role in this process. This –- together with further stabilization of attention – leads to new experiential dimensions of contentment and emotional well-being. Initial brain research supports the trainability of wholesome emotions such as compassion and loving kindness, and we are beginning to understand how such mental training modifies brain function and brain structure. For example, it has been shown that meditators react to emotional prompts of others' distress with heightened activation in brain regions associated with emotion processing, such as amygdala, insula and cingulate cortex (Lutz et al. 2008b).

Finally, when sufficient balance of wholesome motivation, attention and emotional well-being has been developed, the Dzogchen practitioner focuses more closely on an exploration of deeper levels of consciousness beyond the ordinary mind. Such training may involve practices of lucid dreaming and dream yoga, as well as considerations about the transitions of consciousness at the time of death. This leads to longer and more frequent glimpses of the unchangeable, cognizant, luminous, spacious and non-conceptual quality of the mind. This is the time to learn about qualities of the enlightened mind which we will discuss in this book according to traditional Tibetan Buddhist writings on the five types of wisdom awareness. The lasting impact of these advanced subtle explorations of consciousness on the mind and brain is unknown. It is perhaps likely that these practices lead to modifications in synchronicity of oscillations between regions and their interactions, modifying the default state of the brain.

The pyramid of the four levels of mind training corresponds to the gradual progression of practices in the Dzogchen tradition – it represents the fact that each level builds on the previous ones. However, the four levels should not be viewed as static building blocks since they interact with each other and as a result development at one level can bootstrap development on other levels. There is a minimal level of stability which needs to be achieved at each level before one can work efficiently at the next level of the pyramid, but at the same time each level is further cultivated and refined with the development of other levels.

For example, when we work at the emotional level, we will most likely also consider where the training in emotional balance is to lead us, why we are engaging in the practice in the first place. If our motivation is mostly hedonistic and we wish to develop skills at the emotional level in order to be more successful in our work and to appear more attractive to others, the depth of our practice at the emotional level will be greatly limited. It will not resonate with the basic approach of the contemplative training and therefore practices aiming to develop compassion or loving kindness will simply miss the target; they will not make sense from the hedonistic perspective. The quality of our training at the emotional level will also be impacted by the stability of our attention. If our attention is fleeting and we are not able to observe patterns in our mind and monitor how our emotional reactions unfold, it will be virtually impossible for us to apply meditation methods aiming to reduce negative emotions such as anger. This is because we will not be able to notice as the anger unfolds in our mind and by the time we become aware that we are angry the whole chain of emotional events leading up to the feeling of anger would have manifested. At that point we will not really be able to work with the emotion effectively, and our emotion regulation will be more or less limited to 'damage control'.

At the same time, as we develop our skills at each of the levels, our practice involving the other levels will be enhanced as well. If we come back to the example of cultivating compassion, when we experientially expand the scope of our compassion towards all living beings, our motivation may progress from the initial wish for eudaimonic happiness for ourselves, our family and friends to a more encompassing intention for all beings to be happy in the genuine sense. The increasing depth of our practice will most likely also create more zest in our meditation and enable us to concentrate in a sustained manner for longer. At the most advanced level, experiential understanding of all-encompassing compassion will lead to new insights into the nature of the mind and guide our explorations of consciousness to new discoveries.

Intention behind the practice

Intention is central to human behavior. Intentions can be conscious, such as the goal of a student to get to medical school, or unconscious, having their roots in our childhood, forgotten or suppressed memories, or defense mechanisms of our consciousness. Going back to Viktor Frankl, the 'will for meaning' in life arises from intention as the basic feature of the human mind – our actions and behaviors are naturally directed by intentions.

Despite being fundamental to human nature, the notion of intention or motivation for practice is often neglected and sometimes viewed as controversial in current discussions about meditation. In contrast, in the Buddhist context intentions behind our actions, behaviors, thoughts, and speech are the essential determinants of whether our meditation practice is considered virtuous or not (Patrul Rinpoche 1998). In other words, the intention with which we practice influences whether the meditation practice actually contributes to our suffering or leads to liberation from it. For example, if somebody decides to learn meditation in order to gain more attentional focus and endurance in his work, which involves unethical ways to gain money from the stock market, from the Buddhist point of view the practice of meditation actually deepened the person's suffering rooted in his confused vision of happiness. So if meditation practice is used for hedonistic, ego-centered reasons, its outcomes, and the practice itself, are tainted by the wrong view. For a Buddhist practitioner, the intention to attain freedom from suffering supported by deep understanding of the origins of suffering and paths to liberation is the foundation of their practice. In Mahāyāna, Tibetan Buddhism and Dzogchen this intention to attain enlightenment is closely intertwined with the wish to help all sentient beings to attain the same. The achievement of enlightenment is the necessary prerequisite for being able to help others since the highest accomplishment of human potential provides the wisdom and compassion of the mind needed for effectively guiding others on the path to liberation.

In Buddhism, the intention of embarking on the path of mind training is to gain freedom from suffering in its deeper sense. The intention evolves and gains in depth and sincerity as one spends more time in contemplation and experiential meditation practice. Based on where we are with our practice, intention can take on different forms, ranging from an initial yearning for a deeper purpose in life, through search for well-being and balance, up to the highest aspirations of being of service to others through reaching enlightenment. Setting aside such variations for a moment, we can perhaps say that the foundation of the Buddhist path is in ethical intentions. For this reason contemplations about the meaning of happiness and suffering are typically the first practices a Buddhist trainee engages in.

Nevertheless, from a different perspective, the notion of intention linked to virtue and non-virtue may seem quite conventional. It can be viewed as contradictory to the explorative, open-minded and non-judgmental approach cultivated in meditation. Let's consider, for example, secular mindfulness-based approaches where the concepts of non-judgment, acceptance and letting go of goal-oriented attitudes arise as much more prominent than considerations about intention. This is the case in spite of some secular conceptions of mindfulness acknowledging the importance of intention behind practice and even singling it out as one of the components of mindfulness (Shapiro et al. 2006). The intention of meditation practice in secular approaches of mindfulness is not an explicit focus of the training and most people enter mindfulness courses with the simple intention of improving their ability to cope with stress, illness or pain. Perhaps as their practice evolves further, their personal vision and intention behind the practice expand as well. In her study of meditation practitioners, Shapiro (1992) outlined the development of intention from self-regulation, through self-exploration to self-liberation. It is possible that some practitioners of secular mindfulness-based approaches proceed towards this deepening of intention. At some point in this process of intention refinement they will most likely reach out to the traditional Buddhist teachings in order to progress further. This is because secular approaches to mindfulness, as useful as they are in bringing the benefits of certain meditation practices to broad audiences, do not contain teachings and practices covering the whole Buddhist path to liberation, particularly when it comes to the levels of the pyramid of mind training concerned with intention and exploration of consciousness.

Coming back to the controversial role of intention in meditation, when we turn to Dzogchen, the dichotomy of virtue and non-virtue as opposites can seem contradictory to the very concept of non-duality principal to Dzogchen. In fact, many teachings and practices of Dzogchen encourage the practitioner to let go of dichotomies such as 'good–bad', 'suffering–no suffering', even 'meditation–non-meditation'. So how is it possible to discuss virtuous intention while setting aside dichotomies? This can become a source of confusion and misinterpretation unless the discussion is grounded in the broader context of Dzogchen training, which has its roots in Buddhist ethics. Here it is important to emphasize that advanced teachings of Dzogchen challenging and surpassing dichotomies are intended for practitioners who have deeply understood through their study and experiential practice the meaning of suffering and its roots, stabilized their mind to a high level and embody the sincere motivation to free oneself from suffering for the benefit of all beings. In terms of the pyramid of mind training in Dzogchen, letting go of dichotomies falls under the final level of practices exploring the nature of mind, after mastery at the more foundational levels has been achieved. So, while their minds are firmly grounded in their compassionate intention to let go of ego-centered tendencies and to attain enlightenment, practitioners gradually release the superficial dichotomies of the habituated mind in order to realize the ultimate nature of the mind beyond subject–object restrictions. Once they realize the nature of the mind and stabilize their mind in that state continuously, there is no need for conceptual reminders of virtue and non-virtue, suffering and freedom from suffering. The ultimate understanding of ethics arises naturally as part of the experiential realization of the nature of the mind.

Dzogchen masters warn of the dangers of abandoning the foundations of ethics too soon when practitioners mistakenly think they have realized the ultimate nature of the mind whereas in reality they have only experienced first fleeting glimpses of this state or even mistaken experiences of attentional stability for the nature of the mind. Padmasambhava (1999: 100), the foremost master of Dzogchen, described this point as follows:

> some people will indulge in coarse negative emotions, because of not recognizing ego-clinging and failing to diminish their conceptual thoughts. Professing to hold the ultimate view, they will claim that being careful about the effects of virtuous and evil actions is a low view.

This exemplifies why non-duality and the place of ethics within Dzogchen need to be considered in the broader context of sensitivities to the differences between levels and accomplishments in mind training. In sum, letting go of considerations involving ethics, intention and virtue is reserved for the most advanced stages of the final level of mind training and these factors of motivation are indispensable earlier on the path.

Perhaps the key to finding the right place for intentional and ethical aspects of meditation in the context of Buddhist and secular meditation practices in the West is in their explorative, contemplative and experiential nature. Just as with any other Buddhist teachings, Buddhist masters across lineages invite students to consider our intentions and motivation in relation to happiness and suffering. Maybe we can start by asking questions about the differences in the state of our mind in connection to our motivation and intentions. Are we engaging in our meditation practice so that we feel less stressed, because we are searching for deeper meaning in life or out of sheer curiosity? Are there glimpses of search for truth and exploration of who we are and how can we be of ultimate service to others?

Practice: Working with intention

Let's start by settling our body in a straight but relaxed body posture. You may want to review the description of the basic meditation posture from Chapter 1. Once you find a comfortable meditation position, it may be helpful briefly to scan your body from your head to your feet to notice whether you are holding tension in some muscle groups. If you notice tightening of any muscles, for example in your shoulders or your jaw, try to release the tension gently. Sometimes it is useful consciously to tighten the tense muscles even more and then relax them.

Intention to stay focused

Everything we do starts with an intention, whether the intention is conscious or not. You might find it useful to dedicate a minute at the beginning of your meditation session to making a conscious decision that you will allow yourself to spend the following 20 minutes, or whatever the length of your session might be, focusing on your practice. You can simply say to yourself: 'For the next 20 minutes I can stay fully focused on the meditation. I have time to take care of other things later on.' This can help to reduce distraction from thoughts about things you need to do and activities you engaged in earlier.

Five deep breaths and releasing tension

As described in Chapter 1, it is good to center the body and mind using a few mindful deep in-breaths and out-breaths. You may want to go back to the instructions in the first chapter to remind yourself of this practice.

Intention for your practice

The following questions are intended to help you explore aspects of motivation in your life and intention for your meditation practice. You may progress through the questions gradually in your meditation session, or only focus on questions which you feel are more relevant to your experience. You may pause for several minutes, or as long as you wish, to contemplate on these aspects of your motivation. You may also consider just one of them at the beginning of every meditation session. While this meditation is mostly analytical, involving directed thinking, it also contains training in attention. When you notice that the focus of your considerations has diverged to some other thoughts not directly related to the topic of intention, simply come back to the level of motivation you were considering last. It is important to maintain an open-minded, non-judgmental attitude while engaging in this practice. It is not about competitive evaluation of where we stand on the axis of motivation. It is about learning how motivation influences our practice and how we can work on it in order to enhance our meditation.

You may want to start by contemplating the aspects of human potential we have discussed in this chapter and relating them to your own experience. Perhaps you can bring to mind the hierarchy of human needs and explore the levels of motivation from your personal perspective. Do you find that currently your life priorities lie with your friends or family, or maybe with your needs for recognition, or both? Do you think that some of your goals or activities which bring you contentment could reflect your needs of self-actualization? Are there aspects of your life which connect with the self-transcendence element of your experience? Are you able to recognize the shift in the ego-centered perspective towards a 'being' mode of awareness when you consider self-transcending experiences? Moving towards a more subtle distinction in your experience, can you recognize some differences between the conceptual mode of awareness when you are thinking about self-transcending experiences and a more experiential 'being' mode of awareness when you are actually experiencing self-transcendence?

If you like, you may explore now the aspects of motivation and intention specific to meditation training. What brought you to meditation practice? For many, it is experience of suffering in its varied forms, maybe a physical illness, painful chronic condition, stress or loss. Are you practicing mainly to be able to deal with physical and mental challenges better? Do you wish to enhance your well-being through the meditation practice? Or maybe you are simply curious to learn about meditation practice and open-minded about its effects on your life. Is there perhaps also an element of self-exploration you can identify as driving your practice? Is there a wish to learn about yourself, your mind, your purpose in life? Progressing on to the more encompassing aspects of motivation, do you find aspects of concern for others to be motivating your practice as well? Maybe you would like to find ways to be happy in the genuine sense yourself and also wish the same for others. It is possible that your practice inevitably encompasses considerations of happiness and compassion for yourself and others, and you recognize the intertwined shared nature of human experience. Does any aspect of your practice also entail contemplations on the ultimate liberation from suffering as considered in the Buddhist context? Are these considerations quite abstract or is there an experiential element and a sense of achievability of freedom from suffering?

Now you may want to continue with the contemplations on happiness, impermanence, suffering, and gratefulness from the first chapter and other meditation practices. At the end of your session you may want to observe whether your initial considerations about motivation and intention impacted on your consequent practice in the session. You may explore in your own experience motivation as the foundation of any meditation practice.

Summary: Chapter 2

Western psychology describes a progression and development of human needs on the path to fulfillment of one's potential. The hierarchy of human needs starts with basic physical needs of food, water and shelter and culminates with self-actualization in which our skills and talents are fully developed. Some psychologists emphasize a level of needs and motivation beyond the self-actualization. This level transcends the self-centered perspective of happiness and leads one to find deeper meaning and purpose in life beyond the individual. In Buddhism, the fulfillment of human potential means achievement of the highest level of mental balance which encompasses most subtle levels of non-self-centered happiness. It also eliminates completely ordinary experiences of suffering which we often view as inseparable from the human condition.

In Dzogchen, this intricate rebuilding of the human mind corresponds to rewiring and enhancement of four levels of mind and brain. It starts with examination of our motivation and purpose in life, with a review of what makes us genuinely happy. The second level of training stabilizes and refines attention. As we begin to attend to the inner life of our mind more closely, we often notice that it is rather chaotic. It easily and automatically casts judgments about events and experiences which enter our field of attention. In this way our mind continuously oscillates between craving and rejection of what we experience. The task is to gain more understanding of how these automatic reactions influence our life and then we can redirect the mind gently towards well-being enhancing mental activity. At the same time we start developing more patience and friendliness towards ourselves and others. This gives us the courage to explore the mind further and to see clearly the negative habits of the mind and recognize that they can be let go of. The third level is a radical remake of our mind in which we reduce its automatic engagement in negative emotions and cultivate emotions such as compassion and loving kindness instead. This, together with attentional training, deepens the experience of genuine happiness. We discover new dimensions of contentment and emotional well-being. Finally, when a sufficient degree of wholesome motivation, attentional stability and emotional well-being has been developed, we can focus more closely on exploration of what is behind the ordinary mind. We gradually experience longer glimpses of the stable, cognizant, luminous, spacious and non-conceptual quality of our mind which was always there.

At each of the four levels, this mind training differentially modifies the brain. Based on neuroscientific research on meditation available so far, such changes seem to range from strengthening of areas associated with cognitive control, mostly in the prefrontal cortex, to effective down-regulation of brain regions linked to processing of fear and anxiety (e.g., amygdala). Our understanding of changes at the highest levels associated with exploration of consciousness and insight into the nature of mind is currently very limited, but it is likely to involve a shift in synchronicity of oscillations between brain regions.

Chapter 3

Attention training

Science and Buddhism: Attention training and well-being

Every day, in every moment our brains are bombarded by an overload of information. Consider, for example, all the things you could be paying attention to right now. There are probably many different objects in the environment around you. You could be focusing on the shape or color of the chair you are sitting on; you could be paying attention to the space you are in, its color, smell, level of noise and brightness; you could easily shift your focus to a conversation of other people in the background or music playing in the room next door. You could also decide to focus on something not immediately in your field of perception and bring to your mind memories of your last holiday or try to visualize the image of your best friend. In sum, there is a myriad of sensations, perceptions, thoughts and feelings you could be focusing on every second.

If we wanted to take in all the information that the environment and our mind offer at each moment in time, we would inevitably end up with an overwhelming information flood. In addition, an indiscriminate intake of information would result in disjointed, and thus not very useful, mental patterns. Simply put, there is much more information around us and in our brain than we are able to take in and represent in a meaningful way. Psychologists termed this difficulty 'the bottle neck problem' and reasoned that attention is a basic faculty of our mind designed to deal with this issue. Attention helps us select and sustain mental focus on what is relevant to us in each moment, which is only a miniscule fraction of the information available.

Because of its pivotal role in our mental functioning, it is not surprising that attention has been one of the first aspects of cognition studied by psychologists more than 100 years ago. In the current scientific debates about attention, the functions of attention are typically divided into two main subcategories. The first aspect of attention is the general ability to direct attention towards what we need or want to focus on. This function is more or less shared across sensory and perceptual systems, which means that we would rely on mostly the same attention systems regardless of whether we are solving a math problem or listening attentively to a conversation. In contrast, there are more specialized attention systems dedicated to restricted types of stimuli – separate systems attending to sounds, images, smells, touch and, to some extent, emotions. Despite this conceptual division, in our everyday functioning the involvement of both the general attention system and the specialized systems is closely intertwined and coordinated. We would rarely find one system to be active in a complete absence of activation of other systems.

Importantly, the involvement of the general and more specialized systems varies with attention training and practice. Research shows that, at the beginning, as we are trying to learn a new skill, we need to engage the general system of attention. Involvement of this system is linked to a more effortful focusing of attention which typically requires conscious focus. For example, if you recall your first driving lesson, you may remember how difficult it was to coordinate the movement of your hands and feet together with awareness of how the car is responding. With practice, the coordination became effortless and automatic systems of attention took over most of the attention demands. You are now mostly unaware of the complex synchronicity of hands, feet and vision you are applying when driving your car.

The progression from conscious effortful engagement of attention to automatic effortless attentional processing has been extensively studied in neuroscience, mostly in vision research. An often-reported pattern of learning-related neural changes shows that the initial task performance requires coordination between general attention systems mostly located in the prefrontal cortex (PFC) and task-specific areas, but after training the task-specific activations start to dominate. This has been labeled the 'scaffolding and storage' hypothesis: whereas the 'scaffolding' work of general attention is needed to cope with a novel task during initial trials, with practice the task execution relies increasingly on learned and stored representations (Petersen et al. 1998).

Interestingly, development of attention skills during meditation training seems to follow similar principles of mental and neural rebuilding. To illustrate this, we can look at a study which examined modifications in brain areas underlying sustained attention – the ability to focus attention on an object continuously for longer periods of time – in advanced Tibetan Buddhist meditators (Brefczynski-Lewis et al. 2007). Amongst other comparisons, the meditators were divided into two small groups which differed by the total amount of time they spend in meditation practice. Participants in the first group dedicated on average 19,000 hours to meditation practice whereas participants in the second group more than twice that (44,000 hours on average). Participants' brains were scanned during a task where they had to focus continuously on a simple visual stimulus and during a rest period. The contrast between focus and rest indicated greater activation in regions associated with sustained attention in the group with fewer hours of meditation practice. This suggests that, with more meditation practice, focusing of attention continuously becomes less effortful and requires less brain resources.

Going back to the general point about the importance of attention to our functioning, it is obvious that the ability to direct and sustain attention is essential to almost every activity we engage in. It plays a particularly important role in the acquisition of new skills such as learning to read, write, juggle or play a piano. Attention is also one of the main determinants of our work performance across professions, from traffic controllers and builders to nurses, engineers, athletes and researchers. Lapses of attention are often responsible for accidents and safety violations. So it is not surprising that a great deal of research has been dedicated to studying the enhancement of work performance through attention training and optimization of attention resources. Such research almost exclusively focuses on how to reduce errors resulting from lapses of attention and how we can focus for longer and perform faster in a task. For the most part, this research is very rarely, if ever, related to well-being. This is one of the main points of divergence between Western scientific and Buddhist views of attention training.

Buddhist attention training

As we have outlined in the pyramid of mind training developed on the path of Dzogchen, the second level in the progression cultivates and refines attentional abilities of the meditation adept. While the balance of motivation and intention for the practice lays overall foundations for the mind training, development of attentional abilities is indispensable for the cultivation of emotional balance and exploration of consciousness. It is clear that the ability to pay attention impacts on our performance at school and work, but why should attention training be of utmost importance to meditation training which cultivates well-being?

Tibetan Buddhist teachings often use the analogy of an untamed wild horse when explaining the importance of attention to our mental balance. Just like a wild horse, without attention training the mind goes wherever the imminent impulse of attention takes it; we are not really able to guide the mind and often don't even notice that it is out of control. In such a state, the mind is easily distracted by whatever enters its field of perception and follows more or less randomly whatever attracts its attention in the moment. You may want to explore this in your own experience if you simply pause for a moment, maybe just for one minute, and observe how your attention focus shifts, often quite randomly, from one thought or perception to another.

At a more obvious level, we can take the amount of multitasking we do most of the time as an indicator of how scattered our attention is. You may recognize a common scenario: a woman is sitting at her desk, trying to focus on the task in front of her, just to get distracted by the office phone and then a text message, an e-mail she needs to answer immediately, and then a colleague comes in asking some questions. And many of us find it irresistible to start the day by checking e-mails, social networking sites, and the news. We feel rushed most of the time and try to get through all our tasks at hand as fast as we can, just to prepare another 'to do list' when we are finished.

In this way of functioning, it is easy to slip into a mode of responding, in which reactions of like and dislike arise automatically without our awareness and without the option to choose how we actually want to respond. As a result, we may slip into automatic patterns of reacting, some of which might be quite unhealthy. For example, in response to a request to complete a task at work we may automatically react with anxiety and start a cycle of thoughts of self-doubt instead of focusing on the task at hand. In a more personal context of our relationships, we may immediately react to difficulty with frustration rather than trying to find constructive ways to solve the problem. Over years we solidify these patterns of reactivity up to the point where they become largely unconscious; we may not be aware that we always react in the same ways in response to certain triggers. We do not realize that we actually have a choice and do not need to follow the unwholesome automatic mental habits again and again.

This is where training in attention is of utmost importance and relevance to well-being. The aim of attention training in the meditation context is not to be able to do more in less time but actually the opposite. The goal is to create more mental space, to learn to pause, to slow down, to let go of the indiscriminate reactive responding to whatever grabs our attention in the moment. Paradoxically, research shows that attention training involved in meditation actually does result in better attentional performance on standard psychological and neuroscientific tasks despite this not being its purpose. We will review this research evidence at the end of the chapter when we have learned more about the faculties, qualities and progression of attention training in Dzogchen.

So what does such attention training entail? In general, Buddhist methods of cultivating stable attention typically involve learning to focus on a simple object. This may seem to a novice to meditation an incredibly boring task in comparison to the constant overstimulation our mind receives every day. The objects used to train attention vary across Buddhist traditions. In Theravāda practitioners learn to ground their attention on their own breath. The first time we tune into our breathing pattern it may come as a surprise that we have never really noticed all the sensations in our body associated with breathing. In order to train attention in the Tibetan Buddhist tradition the practitioner would often focus on a statue or an image of a Buddha, recite a mantra or combine visualization and mantra recitation. If practiced in a skillful way, Tibetan Buddhist practices consisting of visualizations and mantra recitation involve much more than attention training and actually work with all the levels in the pyramid of mind training at the same time. Nevertheless, attention training is a central even to these more complex practices. In the Dzogchen tradition, the foundational practices stabilizing attention also involve visualizations and mantra recitations. More advanced practices work more closely with mental patterns unfolding in the mind and use them as a means of developing attention skills whilst also deepening the practitioner's insight into the nature of the mind.

Attention training practices in the Buddhist context are described under the labels 'calm-abiding' or 'shamatha' (Pāli: samatha, Sanskrit: śamatha or shamatha; Tibetan: shyiné). They typically involve cultivation of a set of attentional abilities which include being able to shift attention to the object we want to focus on, staying focused on the object with very little distraction, being able to notice when we become distracted and shifting our attention gently back to the object. This description of attentional skills may seem no different from the notions of attention discussed in Western psychology and neuroscience we have discussed earlier. Yet, there are at least two aspects of attention training which set the two approaches apart. The differences arise from the intention and the attitude behind the attention training in the two approaches to mind training.

In line with the motivation to enhance our well-being and proceed on the path leading to freedom from suffering, attention training in the

Buddhist context is a tool for stabilizing the mind to the point where we can explore and effectively work with our mental habits. When our attention is more stable, reactive mental activity in our mind settles gradually like sand in a glass of water. With clarity of attention we are able to observe, perhaps for the first time, the automatic mental habits we have followed mindlessly for years. Recognition of these mental patterns is the basis for being able to choose wisely which mental habits are conducive to our happiness and which are not. With such understanding, we are able to proceed to the next level of mind training where we can consciously develop new mental habits supporting cultivation of well-being and let go of mental habits which are not very useful. Stability of attention is thus a necessary prerequisite for the reshaping of our mind and brain for well-being and happiness. This connection between attention and well-being is largely unknown to Western psychology and neuroscience.

The second point of divergence between the psychological or neuroscientific and Buddhist approaches to attention training is the attitude with which one approaches the training. The most common notion associated with any type of training is that it involves hard work and discipline. This certainly is the case for Buddhist meditation training as well, but, in contrast to other types of training, one of the central skills developed in meditation involves learning to be more compassionate, non-judgmental and accepting towards our experience and others. Just as for many other aspects of meditation training, this may at first seem paradoxical and contradictory. How can attentional focus be developed if we are accepting of the fact that our attentional skills are not very good?

The answer rests in a rather subtle understanding of the meaning of acceptance, non-judgment and friendliness, and their place in meditation training. Acceptance is commonly interpreted as involving an element of non-striving, and may be associated with defeat, but this is not how the term is used in the meditation context. Here acceptance means having the courage to recognize how things are in the moment without denial, avoidance or morphing our experience into something else. Acceptance is closely related to non-judgment and friendliness – it would not be very useful to engage in attention training just to beat ourselves up for learning that our attention is scattered and we are not able to focus very well. In this way our attention training would only perpetuate the cycle of frustration and anxiety and make it worse. Non-judgmental attitude means that we are able to recognize when we get distracted and gently bring our mind back to the object of our attention without labeling the fact that we got distracted as bad or saying that we are not good at attention training.

Elaboration of such thoughts would cause a major distraction to our practice and we would lose track of the object of our meditation all together. This goes hand in hand with the development of a friendly, warm, forgiving attitude towards ourselves and others which helps settle the mind by disengaging from the often circular judgments and labels.

Learning about the mind: Mindfulness and meta-awareness

With the explosion of interest in secular mindfulness-based approaches, the concept of mindfulness is quickly making its way into mainstream contexts, from healthcare, to education and workplace. One of the main reasons for this development is that mindfulness has been shown to enhance our abilities to deal with stress more effectively. This link goes back to the mindfulness-based stress reduction (MBSR) program developed by Jon Kabat-Zinn (1990) in the 1970s as a method of improving coping skills of patients with chronic illness. The MBSR is a program consisting of eight weekly sessions (two and a half hours in duration) taught in groups of 20–30 participants and involving daily home practice of guided meditations (approx. 45 minutes per day). The MBSR laid the foundation for other mindfulness-based approaches, most notably mindfulness-based cognitive therapy (MBCT) (Teasdale et al. 2000), which was specifically developed for the treatment of recurrent depression. The connection between mindfulness and reduction in stress is supported by a relatively large body of research evidence which documents that secular mindfulness training leads to a decrease in stress-related variables such as anxiety and rumination (Baer 2003; Hofmann et al. 2010).

Mindfulness is in secular approaches defined as a non-judgmental mode of awareness marked by attentional focus on the present-moment experience (Kabat-Zinn 2003). The attentional focus on the present moment means that we repeatedly bring our attention to what is happening to us right now. This is in contrast to our attention being caught up in habitual thought patterns which often unfold without our awareness and are detached from the present-moment experience. To exemplify the opposite of mindfulness, just recall an occasion when you were at a meeting and you found yourself spacing out and thinking about something other than what was being discussed. Another example of mindlessness is automatic engagement in an activity without noticing what we are doing as if we were on 'autopilot'.

Paying attention to perceptions and sensations immediately available to our senses is mostly what is understood in mindfulness-based approaches under focus on present-moment experiences. The eight-week programs in MBSR or MBCT gradually develop an increased awareness of body sensations, sounds, feelings, and to some extent thoughts. In the development of present-moment focus, secular mindfulness-based approaches emphasize the importance of the non-judgmental attitude. Through guided meditations practitioners learn to bring their attention gently back to the present-moment experience without slipping into judgments about their ability to do so or other self-evaluative thoughts. In addition to developing non-judgmental present-moment mindfulness, programs such as MBSR and MBCT contain therapeutic elements which involve education about stress, group discussion about pleasant and unpleasant experience, guided yoga and tai-chi practices and walking meditation.

Secular programs in mindfulness have their roots in Buddhist mind training methods, but also diverge from the original conceptions. In Buddhism, mindfulness (Pāli: sati; Sanskrit: smṛti; Tibetan: trenba) is typically described as a cognitive faculty which enables the practitioner to sustain attention on the object of meditation (Wallace 1999a; Olendzki 2008). Mindfulness is associated with prospective memory, the ability to remember to pay attention to the object of meditation in the future (Siegel et al. 2008). Mindfulness is distinguished from meta-awareness (Pāli: sampajañña; Sanskrit: samprajanya; Tibetan: shizhin) which is a related, but separate, cognitive faculty. Meta-awareness is the monitoring element of attention, which checks whether we are focusing on the object of meditation or diverged from it. Noticing when we get distracted is a necessary prerequisite for us to be able to bring the attention back to the object of meditation. In attention training mindfulness and meta-awareness work together in the development of an adept's attention skills.

Within Buddhist traditions, mindfulness is an integral part of the mind training, an important piece in the mosaic of mental skills cultivated on the path to enlightenment. Particularly in the Tibetan Buddhist tradition this means that the practice of mindfulness builds on intentional grounding of Buddhist ethics. In Dzogchen, the goal of mindfulness practice is to develop attention to the point where it can be effectively used in the development of emotional balance and exploration of consciousness. In this way, mindfulness is viewed as a tool, one of the faculties to be cultivated on the Buddhist path of mind training, but not its goal.

The concept of mindfulness in the secular traditions can be viewed both as more broad and more narrow if compared with traditional Buddhist views. It is more encompassing because the two cognitive faculties of mindfulness and meta-awareness are typically both included under the secular label of mindfulness. Secular mindfulness practices involve training in monitoring of our experience in order to enhance the awareness of what is happing in our mind and body in every moment. At the same time, the practices encourage development of attentional focus through shifting and sustaining of attention, mostly on sensory experience. Secular mindfulness also includes a certain level of training in emotional balance because, via enhanced awareness of automatic mental habits, it can lead to cultivation of ways of responding and functioning which are more conducive to well-being. It can also initiate some foundational exploration of consciousness, mostly in the sense of contributing to metacognitive insight – a sense of stepping back from automatic thought patterns and understanding that our thoughts are not necessarily accurate reflections of reality (Teasdale et al. 2002). In this way, the scope of secular mindfulness is not limited to attention training.

The narrowing of perspective in secular conceptions of mindfulness arises as a result of them not being part of a mind training system presenting the full path to liberation from suffering. While some secular mindfulness teachers emphasize that mindfulness-based approaches aim to reduce suffering (Kabat-Zinn 2003), suffering here is understood in the more obvious sense as physical and mental illness or difficulty. There is an element of ethics embedded in secular mindfulness-based approaches and their teaching is guided by principles of good practice. In addition, many secular teachers undergo training in one of the Buddhist traditions and their secular teaching and practice of mindfulness reflect their contemplative background. Nevertheless, secular mindfulness courses are not firmly grounded in Buddhist ethics, there is no explicit focus on this aspect of meditation training, and the extent to which the training contains implicit elements of Buddhist ethics depends on the background of the teacher. At the level of attentional training, the secular mindfulness practices aim to develop foundational levels of attentional focus and meta-awareness, but as we will see in the next section where we review stages of Buddhist mindfulness training, they do not provide guidance on the full development of attentional skills.

Stages of training in calm-abiding and the qualities of attention

Tibetan Buddhist tradition contains fine descriptions of the progression of attention training on the Buddhist path and qualities of attention developed in the process. With regard to stability of attention, such training goes much further than the secular mindfulness-based approaches

– refining attention to the point where one is able to focus continuously on an object for hours. While not all of us may desire to go that far in our attention training, it is certainly inspiring and interesting to learn that our attention is trainable to the levels considered unthinkable by most people in the West. Knowing that attention training is not the goal of the Buddhist path, some may also wonder why adepts of meditation would want to develop such subtle levels of attentional skills.

The Buddhist notion of mindfulness, particularly in the Tibetan Buddhist tradition, does not entail the strong emphasis on present-moment sensory experience which dominates secular approaches to mindfulness. The most common approach to the development of attentional skills in the Tibetan Buddhist tradition involves mental training in visualization of sacred images and mantra recitation. In the Dzogchen tradition this would mainly be practices of visualizing sacred syllables, less so deities.

Given that mindfulness-based approaches instruct practitioners to redirect their attention gently away from elaborative thinking, the emphasis on creation of mental images may seem contradictory to the purpose of mindfulness. However, this is not the case if we consider that elaborative thinking applied here is focused and guided. This means that in focusing on a mental image one would also practice disengagement from thoughts and perceptions other than the object of meditation when distraction arises. Practitioners would engage in these practices with a non-judgmental approach by letting go of labeling their experience and abilities as good or bad, successful or not. There are additional spiritual dimensions to the visualization practices used in Dzogchen which we will leave for a later discussion.

Because of the emphasis on visualization in the Tibetan Buddhist tradition of attention training, the descriptions of the stages of shamatha developed in this tradition have been formulated from the perspective of visualization practices. Nevertheless, the outline of the stages of attention training is equally applicable to attention training with other objects such as the breath. The differences in the object of meditation would lead to some deviations in the experience of the practitioner but the general progression through the stages of attention refinement would be maintained.

Over the last two decades attention training in shamatha has been investigated, detailed and popularized by a Tibetan Buddhist scholar and teacher Alan Wallace (1999a, 2006), who himself underwent extensive training in these practices. The following outline is mostly based on his work:

1. Mental placement: The calm-abiding training in the Tibetan Buddhist tradition starts with observing and memorizing a sacred image one wants to hold and then visualizing the image repeatedly in the mind without a direct visual aid. In the first stage the practitioner can hold the image only for a very short time, perhaps one or two seconds, and then loses the focus completely with thoughts and images unrelated to the visualization interfering. The practitioner notices only after a short while, perhaps after about ten seconds, that the mind has been distracted. Then the practitioner gently brings the attention back to the visualization for a second or two before losing the focus again.

2. Continual placement: With more practice, the stability of practitioners' attention increases and at the second stage they are able to focus on the meditative object for about a minute without getting completely distracted, without noticing this. However, the visualization lacks clarity, which means that the practitioner is not able to visualize details of the image very clearly.

3. Patched placement: At the third stage, the practitioner is able to sustain focus on the object of meditation for at least half an hour and up to an hour. During this time, the practitioner sometimes gets distracted and forgets the object of meditation, but notices this quickly and comes back to the visualization right away. The moments of gross distraction are not very frequent. However, the focus on the meditative object is not completely stable, the practitioner may notice chatter in the background of the mind. In addition, the visualization is still not very clear.

4. Close placement: With an increasing amount of practice, the practitioner is able to stabilize attentional focus to a higher degree. Distraction in meditation arises very rarely, but as a result, the practitioner may slip into the opposite extreme — laxity. This means that the practitioner would hold the visualization continuously, but it would lose detail, becoming foggy and dull. The practitioner may even dose off for a few seconds with or without noticing, then come back to the visualization.

5. Taming: At this stage the main task is to overcome the laxity in meditation by increasing focus on details of the meditative object. The danger at this stage is that the practitioner will confuse the laxity of meditation for advanced stages of meditative stabilization. It is important to remedy this through increased clarity of the visualization.

6. Pacification: Major slips into dullness and laxity are quite rare at this stage. Instead, there are moments of subtle laxity when the

visualization does not have the full clarity of detail. The main task is to increase the clarity or vividness of the visualization further so that even the subtle experience of dullness is minimized.

7. Complete pacification: Further refinement of attentional skills comes through improvement in meta-awareness up to the point where very short and very subtle moments of dullness and distraction are readily detected and countered through swift return to the meditative object. As a result, vividness and clarity of the visualization are enhanced to a high degree.

8. Single-pointed placement: The practitioner is now able to focus on the meditative object continuously and almost completely without interference from even very subtle dullness or distraction. Because of the stability of focus, meta-awareness is rarely needed for monitoring of changes in the focus. Increased reliance on meta-awareness may actually disrupt the continuous state of attentional focus by shifting attention away from the object of meditation and towards monitoring.

9. Balanced placement: One-pointed focus can now be sustained for hours and requires very little effort. The practitioner experiences deep levels of peace and subtle joy while in the meditative state. According to Wallace (2006), achievement of the highest level of stability in shamatha is an actual event marked by powerful shifts in bodily energies. This results in experience of ecstatic joy which is neither lasting nor the goal of the training, but is a sign of accomplishment. After this event the mind settles in a stable, peaceful, and subtly joyful state of mental pliancy. The mind is now fully serviceable for other practices of deepening emotional balance and exploring the nature of the mind and reality.

Along the progression through the nine stages of shamatha, the practitioner develops three qualities of attention: relaxation, stability and clarity (Wallace 2006). Relaxation means releasing tension in the mind and body, stability describes continuity of focus and clarity is about vividness of the meditative object. Often the main difficulties the practitioner faces at the beginning of attention training are tension and overemphasis on discipline. This is perhaps particularly an issue for practitioners in the West because a lot of our schooling and work teaches us that we just need to 'try harder' in order to achieve the goal. Following the same approach, many meditation beginners start by building up tension in their body and mind through arduous copying of meditation postures of advanced masters and sitting through their practice 'no matter what' for a specific amount of time every day. This approach may work to some extent at the very beginning and the attention skills may improve a bit, but after a while the practitioner starts to stagnate in the practice. The reliance on sheer discipline also leads to the practice not being very enjoyable. Not surprisingly, many beginners who apply this approach would practice for a couple of months and then abandon the practice altogether. Some practitioners stick to their meditation practice despite this and as a result can spend years in meditation training without really progressing. It is important to realize early on that the goal-oriented approach based on sheer discipline does not work for meditation training, including training in attention, and we need to start with relaxation.

To counter the tension, goal-oriented attitude and overreliance on discipline the practitioner first learns to notice the tension in the body and mind, and then applies techniques to balance the body and mind. This may involve breathing and yoga practices which calm down and relax the body and mind and in this way prepare for meditation. The practitioner would also learn to let go of mental tension through development of a non-judgmental attitude. Just like in secular approaches to mindfulness, the non-judgmental attitude would also involve an element of self-compassion, development of patience and friendliness towards ourselves and our own experience. The overcritical attitude is one of the main problems of people in Western cultures and is instrumental in anxiety-related illness and depression. For many practitioners it is very easy to slip into the 'I can't do this, I am not good at this' mode when starting with meditation. The non-judgmental attitude and self-compassion become essential tools to counter the habit of being unhelpfully critical and judgmental.

The second quality of attention developed in shamatha is stability and can simply be described as the ability to maintain the focus of attention on the object of meditation. As we can see in the outline of the stages of shamatha, stability of attention gradually develops from focusing for a second or two in the first stage up to the level of one-pointed focus sustained for hours in the final stages. This clearly exemplifies trainability of sustained attention to very high levels and initial research supports this. The Shamatha project (www.shamatha.org) led by Cliff Saron and Alan Wallace followed cognitive and neural changes in multiple aspects of attention processing in practitioners undergoing training in shamatha for three months. As part of the project the practitioners trained for approximately five hours a day in a retreat environment. The results showed improvement in the ability to sustain attention (MacLean et al. 2010).

The last quality developed in shamatha is clarity of meditative focus. This describes the ability to visualize clearly with as much detail as possible the image the practitioner holds in the mind. If the practitioner focuses on a concrete object such as breath, clarity of focus would mean being able to attend to details of the perceptions and hold them. In this way a practitioner may start by noticing major abdominal movement when observing the breath, but with increased attentional focus starts attending to more subtle perceptions, for example at the nostrils. Coming back to visualizations, the mental image at the beginning of attention practice is typically very blurry. In the advanced stages the practitioner is able to maintain focus on the visualization with all the intricate details in the front and in the background. Clarity or vividness in meditation is an antidote to laxity, but enhancement of vividness can sometimes result in increased excitability, manifesting as interference from unrelated thoughts and images. In this sense, the practitioner may feel that, after achieving a high degree of stability in the practice, increase in vividness is bringing them one step back to the less refined states of stability. This should, however, be only a temporary setback until the practitioner finds new levels of balance between stability and vividness in the practice.

Now that we have discussed the qualities of attention, it is also interesting to explore the interplay of reliance on mindfulness and meta-awareness in the development of shamatha. A beginner typically shows very low levels of mindfulness in the sense of being able to sustain attention on the object of meditation. While the adept trains the stability of attention, the main task is to notice distraction as quickly as possible and bring the attention back to the object of meditation. This means that training in mindfulness goes together with reliance on meta-awareness which may actually dominate the training at the initial stages. This is because, without the ability to monitor the status of attention, increased mindfulness cannot be achieved. With increased proficiency in meta-awareness, the stability of mindfulness is enhanced as well up to the point where the need for reliance on meta-awareness decreases. At the highest stages, the involvement of meta-awareness can even be counterproductive because it can interfere with the highly stable focus on a meditative object and become a distraction in itself.

Finally, we may ask whether it is really possible to achieve the highest stages of shamatha and if so, how long it would take. According to traditional Buddhist sources (Wallace 2006), it takes three to nine months of full-time training in retreat to achieve shamatha. It is not clear whether these assessments would hold for practitioners in the West – up until now there are no recorded cases of Westerns accomplishing the highest stage of shamatha. Even if the training required one or two years, to many Westerners it will come as a surprise that such high levels of attentional focus are at all possible and achievable by training. One or two years of daily practice may actually not seem too excessive if we consider how long it takes to achieve high levels of mastery in any kind of skill, including athletic performance or learning new languages. The main difference in the case of meditative attention training is that the skills acquired are oriented inwardly, towards enhancement of the balance and well-being of the mind.

How does meditation training modify the systems of attention?

The nascent nature of research into cognitive and neural changes associated with meditation training is reflected in the relatively small number of studies which investigated changes in attention as a result of training in calm-abiding practices. Yet, attentional skills seem to be more malleable to scientific examination because of relatively clear delineation between practices of focused meditation and other meditation techniques targeting attention (Lutz et al. 2008a). Before we turn to the research evidence, let's briefly explore research methods used to investigate the effects of meditation training on the mind and brain.

Research methods used in investigating the mind and brain

The vast majority of experimental research examining function of the mind and brain relies on computerized reaction time techniques. For example, a participant could be sitting in front of a computer screen watching a fast-paced sequence of letters and numbers presented on the display. The task might be to respond whenever a number appears on the screen. Given that numbers are presented much less often than letters, this requires strong attentional focus and alertness from the research participant. The researcher could measure both how fast the participant responds (reaction time) and the number of correct responses (accuracy) and missed trials. If we expect the attentional skills to improve following meditation training, we would most likely predict that meditators should show higher accuracy and faster reaction times than people not trained in meditation (if the two groups are matched for important variables such as age, gender, cognitive disability).

Reaction time and accuracy measures build the foundation for other experimental methods assessing functioning of the mind and brain, most notably those used in cognitive neuroscience. The most common methods of neuroscience rely either on electroencephalograhy (EEG) or magnetic resonance imaging (MRI). EEG records electrical activity of the brain (on the scale of microvolts) in the form of oscillations reflecting firing of neural assemblies. EEG recordings can also be used to derive so-called event-related potentials (ERPs) – averaged brain waves elicited by a stimulus (such as a letter or number in a task we have described above). ERPs have excellent time resolution; they are able to record the brain's electrical activity with a millisecond accuracy. However, they do not provide very specific information regarding the actual neural generators of the electrical signal. This is because of the uneven curved surface of the brain with neurons located in varied orientations to the surface of the skull. In contrast, methods such as functional magnetic resonance imaging (fMRI) have very good spatial resolution (in terms of millimeters), but relatively poor timing specificity. fMRI is based on metabolic changes in the blood (blood oxygenation level-dependent (BOLD) signal) in response to cognitive demands which require time, causing a few seconds' delay in responding to a stimulus. In addition to fMRI, there are other methods based on MRI which can measure changes in the brain's structure (e.g., voxel-based morphometry) or neurotransmitters in the brain (magnetic resonance spectroscopy).

The research evidence

It may be useful to divide the research studies available so far along two axes. One of the axes stands for the type of focused meditation training practiced by participants in the study. Here we can find studies of practitioners trained in the Tibetan Buddhist tradition of shamatha (Brefczynski-Lewis et al. 2007; Kozhevnikov et al. 2009; MacLean et al. 2010), adepts in the tradition of Theravāda (Slagter et al. 2007; Cahn and Polich 2009; Lutz et al. 2009) and practitioners of secular mindfulness-based approaches (Jha et al. 2007; Jensen et al. 2012). The other axis could designate whether the experimental task required participants to engage in a meditative state while performing the task (Brefczynski-Lewis et al. 2007; Cahn and Polich 2009) or not (Lutz et al. 2009; MacLean et al. 2010). This is an important aspect of the assessment because it taps into the question whether meditation changes our functioning inside and outside meditation sessions. It is possible that the positive effects of meditation are restricted to the meditation sessions, last while we are meditating, but do not really affect the mind and brain when we are not in the meditative state.

With regard to the effects of meditation training outside meditation sessions, it has been shown that three months of shamatha training in retreat (approximately five hours a day) lead to improvement in the ability to sustain attention (MacLean et al. 2010). The research study used a reaction time task which required participants to follow a fast presented sequence of long and short lines on the computer screen. They had to respond to short lines which appeared less frequently (only 10% of cases). The research showed an improvement in the detection rates (accuracy) and faster reaction times after the retreat.

A similar finding was previously obtained in a study with Theravāda practitioners tested before and after three months of training in retreat (Slagter et al. 2007). This study used a task similar to the one we have described above, with letters and numbers presented in a fast sequence. In addition to a simple detection of rare stimuli, the task also assessed so-called 'attention blink'. Attention blink means that if two stimuli we need to respond to occur too close together in time (within 500 ms), we often cannot see the second target. In other words, detection of the first target taxes our attentional resources to the point where there is not much attention left for detection and responding to the second target. The study found that meditators were able to respond faster and with higher accuracy to the targets after the retreat and this also held for the not-easy-to-detect stimuli presented during the attentional blink. In addition to reaction time and accuracy measures, this study also used ERPs and found a decrease in voltage in an ERP component sensitive to attention. The decrease in voltage went together with a higher detection of the attention blink targets. This was taken as evidence that meditators are able to use limited attentional resources more efficiently.

The notion of better use of attentional control is further supported by research with advanced meditators tested in tasks involving mental imagery. Expert Tibetan Buddhist meditators who had ten or more years of meditation experience in visualization practices were tested before and after 20 minutes of visualization. The purpose of the study was to examine the effects of visualization practice on systems of attention associated with visuospatial memory, ability to remember new visual images unrelated to meditation (Kozhevnikov et al. 2009). Interestingly, the study found that the meditators trained in visualization performed better on the new visualization task after the visualization practice. The authors suggested that this could be due to the visualization practice enhancing attention abilities which in turn improve efficient use of working memory for images.

Other studies examined the brain reactions to distracters while expert meditators were engaging in focused meditation. A study with Tibetan Buddhist practitioners using fMRI found less activation in regions associated with random brain activity and more activation in areas linked to focused attention and inhibition of distraction (Brefczynski-Lewis et al. 2007). Similarly, an ERP study with experienced Theravāda practitioners compared their brain responses to simple tones aimed to distract them while they were in meditation and outside of meditation (Cahn and Polich 2009). The results showed a significant decrease in ERP potentials associated with attentional startle reactions while the practitioners engaged in meditation. This effect was stronger for participants with more meditation training.

While these effects are impressive, many adepts of meditation ask whether less intense meditation training can also improve attention skills. Secular mindfulness-based approaches entail a strong emphasis on shifting of attention to the present moment, mostly immediate sensory experience, so it is interesting to examine whether this less demanding type of training modifies systems of attention as well. Initial evidence comparing the performance of participants new to meditation before and after eight weeks of MBSR training suggests that this type of training also improves the ability to sustain attention (Jha et al. 2007) and select relevant information (Jensen et al. 2012). The study conducted by Jensen et al. (2012) provides particularly powerful evidence because it compared participants trained in MBSR with control participants who received training in all elements of MBSR other than actual mindfulness training. In other words, the study shows that the improvement in attention in participants trained in MBSR is due to the actual mindfulness practice rather than information on stress reduction or other therapeutic elements of the programme.

Overall, the research evidence available so far clearly shows that meditation-based attention training can improve attention skills. Coming back to the division of attention into the general and more specialized systems, it seems that meditative attention training mostly enhances the domain-general attentional skills. Across studies which involved participants trained in varied meditation practices, from breath focus and attention to sensory experience to visualization, there seems to be agreement that meditation-based attention training improves the efficiency with which we use attentional resources. This convergence probably arises from similarities in the attention functions trained across meditation traditions which include focusing on an object of meditation, monitoring attention and disengaging from distractions. Considering that attention enables us to deal with the bottle neck problem of restricted capacity of the brain to process information, the ability to use the limited attentional resources more efficiently seems to be the key to improvement of our functioning.

There are, of course, some variations in the effects due to the specific training used, such as improvement in visualization-related memory after visualization training (Kozhevnikov et al. 2009) and increase in activation in areas of the brain associated with sensory experience in mindfulness-based meditation practices (Farb et al. 2010; Hölzel et al. 2011a). But if meditation training resulted in improvement of specialized attention systems only, it would make it much less useful to everyday functioning and well-being. For example, it would not be very interesting if training in breath focus made us better at focusing on the breath and nothing else. The improvement in general attentional efficiency reported in the studies we reviewed is likely associated with changes in the PFC such as dorsolateral PFC (Brefczynski-Lewis et al. 2007) and anterior cingulate (Hölzel et al. 2011b). This resonates with accounts of two main systems of executive control associated with detection and monitoring of stimuli (Petersen and Posner 2012) which regulate allocation of attention across different tasks and sensory systems. It is an exciting task for future research to provide a more detailed map of attentional systems of the mind and brain modified by meditation and their modulation by different meditation techniques and stages of attention training.

Practice: Calm-abiding meditation on breath awareness

To release any tension you may be holding, it is good to start your practice by first settling your body in a straight but relaxed posture. You may go back to the practice section in Chapter 1 if you need to review the basic meditation postures in more detail. Once you find a comfortable position, you may want gradually to scan different muscle groups in your body, from your head to your feet, to check if you notice tension somewhere in your body. If you find a muscle group which is excessively tight, you may try to release the tension gently through conscious relaxation. Then you can proceed to the five deep in-breaths and out-breaths which will help you relax further. Make sure that the out-breath is slightly longer than your in-breath; this helps to balance the autonomous nervous system in your body towards relaxation.

In the next step you could bring to your attention the practices focusing on the intention for your meditation from Chapters 1 and 2.

Focusing on your breath

You can now proceed to a short breathing meditation practice. If you are new to meditation and starting with focused meditation training, it is recommended to take a 'low-dose' approach. Practice in a few short sessions, only five minutes in duration, during the day. When the stability of your attention increases, you can extend the duration of your focused attention session accordingly. If you start with long sessions right from the beginning, you will most likely find that you spend most of the session thinking about something else and you are not bringing your attention back to your meditation readily. You may also build up tension in your body.

Now to start the actual practice, you may gently bring your attention to your breath. Breathe naturally and simply pay attention to your breath; you may focus on the movement of your abdomen with your breath, you may focus on the subtle movement of air at your nostrils or follow each breath as it enters and leaves your body. If you notice that your mind wanders away from your breath, bring it gently back without judgment and without elaboration. Just let the mind come back to your breathing and stay with it. Repeat it again and again. Be relaxed but alert; try to notice that your mind is focusing on something other than your breath as soon as possible. If it helps, you can visualize breath moving in a half-circle. As you breathe, in your breath travels down your chest to the area just below your navel. As you breathe out, the air leaves your body, creates a half-circle and stops at the level of your navel outside your body. If you like, you can also count your breaths. You may want to spend the next five minutes focusing closely on your breath in this way.

Summary: Chapter 3

Attention is a basic faculty of the mind, enabling us to deal with constant information overload. Western psychology clearly recognizes the importance of attention to our everyday functioning, but typically links attention training to being able to perform tasks faster and make fewer errors. However, Buddhist teachings emphasize that refined, stable and serviceable attention is actually essential for our well-being. It provides the calm space and stability of focus which enable us to observe the processes of our mind for long enough in order to gain insights into how our mind works. Stability of attention is also linked to emotional well-being. If we are able to manage our attention more efficiently, negative emotions do not overtake our mind easily.

Attention meditation training often starts with bad news when we realize how scattered and unstable our attention is. But after a couple of weeks of regular practice and adjustments to our lifestyle, we may notice that our attentional stability is in much better shape. It may come as a pleasant surprise when we realize that, with a gentle approach and repetition, it is possible to train attention, just like any other skill.

There are two basic faculties of attention developed through such training: mindfulness and meta-awareness. Mindfulness in the Tibetan Buddhist context is the ability to sustain attention on an object such as our breath. Meta-awareness notices any lapses of mindfulness and directs attention back on to the object of meditation. Tibetan Buddhist writings describe a progression of nine stages of attention training corresponding to gradually increasing levels of mental and physical well-being. This process culminates in the ability to sustain attention on an object at will for hours. However, this is not the final goal of meditation training. Stable and refined attention is like a tool which can now be applied in further stabilization and then examination of the nature of the mind in the following steps of the path.

While research into specific changes in the mind and brain resulting from meditation-based attention training is in its infancy, initial studies suggest that meditation training modifies brain regions in the frontal lobes associated with attention control. These changes contribute to more efficient use of brain resources associated with attention which enables meditators to notice more in a shorter time. In addition, meditation practitioners seem to be less sensitive to automatic startle reactions. Hopefully, future research will investigate gradual stages of Buddhist attention training, including very advanced levels of stability, and provide new ground-breaking insights into our abilities to train attention skills related to well-being.

Chapter 4

Emotional balance

Science and Buddhism: What are emotions?

For many of us emotions are what defines the richness of our lived experience. When it comes to meditation and emotions, one of the misconceptions is that meditation practice may flatten the vividness of our emotional experience. On one occasion I had a discussion about meditation and emotional balance with a doctoral student in psychology who was very interested in meditation, but found the idea of letting go of some emotions difficult. He thought that it would be good to cultivate more emotional balance, but at the same time it was hard for him to imagine that he would no longer experience the ups and downs of emotional life, the extremes of excitement, disappointment, pleasure and frustration. For him, the oscillation between pleasure and pain was what life is about, what makes our life interesting. He thought that meditation meant not experiencing these extremes any more, or at least not with such intensity, and this would lead to an impoverished experience of the world. His understanding was that meditation meant sinking into a flat neutral emotional state.

I think the image of a meditator sitting quietly with a subtle smile on his face without being bothered by anything around him sometimes creates the idea of emotional flatness and indifference. This is one of the most common incorrect stereotypes about meditation. As we will see, emotional balance resulting from meditative mind training is anything but an indifferent neutral state of mind. Let's start our exploration by examining what emotions are from the Western scientific perspective and from the Buddhist point of view.

Western scientific views of emotions

Western psychology describes emotions as distinct from other related concepts such as affect and mood (Scherer 1984). 'Affect' is an overarching category which includes emotions, moods, impulses and even stress. Moods, in comparison to emotions, are longer lasting – we can feel the same mood for days or weeks. In contrast, emotions are typically experienced for a shorter amount of time, often in response to a specific event – a student can be upset about a bad grade or on another occasion excited about a birthday party.

When it comes to definitions of emotions, feeling associated with an emotion is often what comes first to our mind. However, scientists define emotions in terms of a broad range of components which include feelings, thoughts, physiological changes in the body and tendencies to act (Scherer 2000; Frijda 2001a). Imagine, for example, an event when you were feeling angry. There was probably a distinct emotional feeling linked to it; it felt different from, let's say, feeling sad or bored. The feeling was probably accompanied by repeated thoughts about the person or event that made you angry. In addition, if you observed changes in your body physiology, you may have noticed faster heart beat and increased sweating. And there might have also been a tendency to respond, perhaps by suppressing the expression of anger so that others would not notice, or by starting a confrontation. This example demonstrates the prevailing view in the current research that emotions are multifaceted phenomena.

Despite this multicomponent view of emotions, emotional experience (feeling) is the aspect of emotion which remains most salient in our everyday encounters with emotions. Emotional experience is often described as different from sensations and perceptions felt through our senses. Unlike sensations, emotions have personal meaning (with respect to our notions of who we are) and are relational (emotions often arise as interplay between us and an event, thing or person) (Frijda 2001b). Definitions of the experiential element of emotions vary across researcher groups. Perhaps the most common view (Scherer 2003) considers emotional experience to be a conscious feeling (we are aware of our emotions) which consists of an integrated representation of changes occurring in other components of emotion. But some researchers object that emotional experience does not necessarily have to be conscious, that we are not always aware of experiencing emotions (Lambie and Marcel 2002; Winkielman and Berridge 2004; Nielsen and Kasczniak 2007).

Even though the experiential side of emotions dominates our understanding of what emotions are, emotional experience as such has been significantly less researched in comparison to other components of emotions (Scherer 2003; Nielsen and Kaszniak 2007). As a result, there is a large body of research on physiological changes associated with emotions, but a striking lack of theories and research on processes that underlie our ability to experience and produce reports about emotional experience. The traditional approach to assessment of emotional experience uses two basic dimensions of emotion – valence and arousal (Bradley and Lang 2000). Emotional valence places an emotion on a scale from positive to negative (pleasant to unpleasant). Arousal, on the other hand, reflects the intensity of emotional experience. Using the two dimensions it is possible to position each emotion in a two-dimensional space of valence and arousal. Anger, for example, would be on the negative side of the valence axis and usually has high intensity. In contrast, feeling bored may be described as a somewhat negative emotion which is low in intensity.

There are also physiological markers of valence and arousal. Researchers have repeatedly demonstrated a close relationship between facial expressions and valence of stimuli. Changes in facial expression can be measured using facial electromyography (EMG), which records modifications in tension of some facial muscles. There are two main facial muscles sensitive to valence – the corrugator supercilii muscle located between the eyebrows which produces frowning and the zygomatic major muscle which controls smiling. When we experience unpleasant emotions (and also moods) there is an increase in the activity responsible for contraction of the corrugator supercilii and little or no change in the zygomatic major muscle. In contrast, pleasant emotions are associated with an increase in the zygomatic major muscle activity and no change or a decrease in the corrugator supercilii tension.

The arousal dimension of emotions also has associated physiological markers, one of them being changes in skin conductance (electrodermal activity). Skin conductance measures modifications in electrical conductivity of the skin which is caused by increases or decreases in skin moisture resulting from sweating. Sweating is an indicator of arousal because changes in skin moisture are controlled by the sympathetic nervous system which activates the fight and flight reaction. Changes in skin conductance are strongly correlated with people's ratings of how intense the emotion feels regardless of the emotion's valence. Higher skin conductance response usually occurs with highly arousing pleasant or unpleasant experience, whereas low skin conductance is recorded to neutral stimuli. There are also other physiological indicators of emotional experience such as changes in heart rate and breathing patterns. For example, anger has been linked to increased heart rate and repeated experience of anger has been shown to result in higher risk of heart arrhythmias (Lampert et al. 2009).

Initial studies also point to a distinct brain circuitry underlying experiences of valence and arousal. A functional magnetic resonance imaging (fMRI) study examined participants' brain responses to positive, negative and neural pictures and words, with positive and negative items being equated for arousal to isolate the two dimensions of emotion (Kensinger and Schacter 2006). The findings showed that high arousal, but not valence, was associated with changes in prefrontal brain regions (dorsomedial prefrontal cortex and ventromedial prefrontal cortex) and also amygdala. In contrast, valence induced differences in activation of other prefrontal regions – the lateral prefrontal cortex was sensitive to negative stimuli and medial prefrontal cortex was activated more strongly in response to positive stimuli. This provides further support in favor of the two-dimensional map of emotions.

Overall, Western research has so far mainly investigated emotions of anger, sadness, disgust, sexual pleasure and hedonistic happiness. In this research the focus has been on physiological, and more recently, brain changes induced by these emotions. Research into emotional experience as such has been mostly limited to participants' ratings of their feelings on scales of valence and arousal. Very few studies examined more subtle emotions, particularly positive emotions, including gratitude, forgiveness and compassion.

Buddhist views of emotions

Surprisingly, there is no separate category called 'emotions' in Buddhist languages including Pāli, Sanskrit and Tibetan (Ekman et al. 2005). This is because Buddhist psychology (Pāli: Abhidhamma; Sanskrit: Abhidharma) does not divide mental processes into categories such as thoughts, emotions and decision making. Rather, it describes mental states which integrate these categories. For example, one of the mental states listed in Mahāyāna Yogācāra Abhidharma texts applied in the Tibetan Buddhist tradition is the affliction of jealousy which manifests itself through a distinct feeling, thoughts, skewed perceptions of other's achievements and actions motivated by the jealousy. While this description of jealousy is somewhat reminiscent of what scientists in the West consider to be components of emotions, Buddhist psychology would not define mental states in terms of their components. However, this is not the main point of departure between Buddhist and Western psychologies

— the essential difference in their views of emotions pertains to how emotions are categorized.

Buddhist psychology (in what follows we focus on the Mahāyāna Yogācāra Abhidharma) divides mental states into afflictive and whole-some. This division is simply based on whether the mental states cause harm or lasting happiness, whether they are sources of suffering or contribute to our well-being and genuine happiness. There are six main afflictive emotions – craving, anger, pride, ignorance/delusion, afflictive doubt and afflictive views (Goleman 2003). These are further divided into 20 derivative mental afflictions such as resentment, cruelty, inflated self-esteem, dullness, blind faith, deception, shamelessness and distraction (Goleman 2003). Turning to the positive side of the spectrum, Buddhist psychology describes wholesome mental states such as the sense of self-respect, conscientiousness, regard for consequence, non-attachment, non-hatred, diligence and equanimity. In addition, the Mahāyāna tradition particularly emphasizes cultivation of four wholesome states associated with mental balance, well-being, and genuine happiness (termed the four immeasurables; Pāli: appamaññā; Sanskrit: apramāṇa; Tibetan: tsad med zhi). These are the qualities of compassion, loving kindness/friendliness, sympathetic joy and equanimity (Wallace 1999b).

In general, the Buddhist approach to emotions highlights the ability of the mind to change its ways, the possibility of consciously and purposefully developing positive mental habits involving wholesome mental states. Development of wholesome emotions is so central to Buddhist mind training, particularly in Mahāyāna, that it is inherent in the progression of the Buddhist path from its beginning. If we look back at the first level in the pyramid of mental states developed in Dzogchen, cultivation of wholesome intentions and motivation involves contem-plations on what aspects of our mental life bring us contentment and which cause harm. From the perspective of Theravāda, this in itself contributes to development of one of the wholesome roots of mental states – non-delusion (Thera 1998). In addition, as a result of contemplations on impermanence we may develop diligence in our practice. Similarly, considerations about genuine happiness may lead to more conscien-tiousness and regard for consequence, and contemplations on deeper sources of suffering can reduce hatred towards those who harmed us.

Cultivation of wholesome mental states is, at least to some extent, also implied in the training of attention. As we have discussed in the previous chapter, non-judgment and self-compassion are mental qualities which help the practitioner counter some of the difficulties in attention training arising from reliance on sheer discipline. Non-judgment, sense of warmth and friendliness towards our experience are actually considered one of the axioms of mindfulness in secular mindfulness-based approaches (Bishop et al. 2004). And Buddhist training in attention in the Tibetan Buddhist tradition often goes hand in hand with explicit training in compassion, loving kindness, sympathetic joy and equanimity. This was, for instance, the case in the Shamatha project where participants primarily trained in attention, but their training was accompanied by the development of wholesome emotions (Jacobs et al. 2011).

Nevertheless, training in emotional balance becomes a full focus of meditation training in Dzogchen only after sufficient stability at the motivational and attentional levels has been achieved. Without a clear understanding of what is genuine happiness and what the practitioner wants to achieve through mind training, it is hard to distinguish between wholesome and afflictive mental states. But the firm foundation of motivation would in itself not be entirely sufficient for effective work at the emotional level. This is because clarity and stability of attention are needed for the mind to settle to the point where the practitioner is able to observe with clarity how the mind works, how it is possible to let go of some mental habits and create new healthier ways of functioning. In the whirlpool of reactive mental activity, it is very difficult to cultivate wholesome mental states because the mind is easily distracted by unrelated thoughts and emotions. Let's now consider the development of the four main wholesome emotions in more detail.

The four healthy emotions

The mind uses a myriad of defense mechanisms which prevent us from facing our anxieties and painful experiences. These are mental strategies which often disguise unhealthy mental habits. Defense mechanisms are sometimes useful – when we are faced with life-changing situations such as receiving a diagnosis of a life-threatening illness or being in a car accident our mind may initially shut down. We may not remember what happened, avoid dealing with the situation or deny that this is happening to us. After the initial shock, the mind may settle to some extent and we may be ready to experience and work with the challenging experiences and emotions. At a more subtle and less dramatic level, the mind uses defense mechanisms to limit exposure to painful experiences such as feelings of anxiety, shame or guilt. For example, a student who receives a bad grade may blame his teacher or circumstances for the outcome instead of recognizing his lack of preparation for the exam. Similar responses to difficult situations may become automatic mental responses which we apply without even noticing.

In order to cultivate emotional balance, practitioners gradually bring such habits to their awareness and develop healthier ways of responding to challenges. It may come as an unpleasant surprise when we learn about our defense mechanisms, and it takes a lot of courage and determination to face the unhealthy habits and develop healthier ways of functioning. There is the need to empower the mind through cultivation of healthy emotions to be able to face the defense mechanisms and to work skillfully with unpleasant or painful experiences. This is where cultivation of qualities of friendliness, compassion, rejoicing and equanimity becomes indispensable and other positive mental states such as forgiveness, gratitude and contentment may naturally follow. Without these wholesome qualities it is easy to slip into denial where we simply do not want to learn about the state of our mind. If this happens, meditation practice may stagnate and it can be difficult to develop well-being and balance further.

Developing a vision: Loving kindness

Common perceptions of loving kindness and compassion may associate these wholesome mental states with a frivolous, even naive attitude to life manifesting through superficial affection towards everything and everybody without discernment. These views omit the important fact that courage, clarity and ability to respond wisely are integral qualities of loving kindness and compassion. Loving kindness (Pāli: mettā; Sanskrit: maitrī) is the wish to be happy in the most wholesome and genuine way we can imagine. The wish for happiness here needs to be placed in the context of Buddhist philosophy – when we talk about happiness we do not mean hedonistic pleasure or simply wishing everybody to get whatever they want. The notions of well-being and genuine happiness are inherent to the concept of loving kindness.

As part of meditation practice it is very useful to develop a vision of happiness we want to follow. Contemplations on loving kindness may connect here with meditations on the meaning of happiness. Practitioners may ask in their practice: What does being happy mean to me? What is the most noble wish I have for myself? What would it be like to achieve advanced levels of mental balance? Contemplations on loving kindness arising from these questions help us consider what the long-term goal of our practice is. As we progress in our meditation, it is good to revisit these contemplations and reflect on our practice. Evolution of a personal vision of happiness often serves as a good indicator of well-being gradients we experience as our mind training moves forward. It can also prevent stagnation in practice. After a couple of years of meditation, it is sometimes easy to slip into a routine and disconnect from the ultimate goal of meditation practice. This loss of vision can stop practitioners from progressing further in their contemplative practice. Loving kindness as a clear personal vision of genuine happiness can help us to maintain a fresh focus in our practice.

The first time we practice meditations on loving kindness, it may feel strange to focus on a wish for our own happiness rather than to wish happiness for others. It may be partially because in the Western culture we are quite used to self-criticism, but rarely consider our own genuine happiness. For this reason it is sometimes easier to start the practice of loving kindness with a focus on the happiness of another person and then expand the circle of contemplation to include ourselves and progress further. The practice of loving kindness – just like practices of compassion, rejoicing and equanimity – involves a progression of meditations on our own happiness, the happiness of those who are close to us, the happiness of people we are neutral to and then happiness for those we have difficulties with.

The notion of wishing happiness for somebody we do not know or a person we have difficulties with may seem very unusual. A neutral person would be somebody we have not met personally, maybe a person who passes by when we are walking down the street. Expanding the wish for happiness to neutral people – people we would usually ignore – aims to melt the artificial divisions between near and far created by our culture and society. It highlights the shared nature of human experience, the fact that, just like us, others are experiencing feelings of anxiety, insecurity, anger, fear and maybe also glimpses of grace, courage and wishes for genuine happiness. From the perspective of Dzogchen, the practices of the four healthy emotions tackle the fundamental duality of our self and the other.

Wishing happiness to our enemies, people we have difficulties with, may at first sound even more striking. But if we consider that genuine happiness means balance of the mind which is free from anger, craving and ignorance, this approach may appear much more rational. If violent and harmful people could experience well-being and genuine happiness, by definition their minds would be free from the anxieties, anger and ignorance which may translate into actions of harm. In this way, the wish for our own genuine happiness together with the same wish for everybody can become very healing to our immediate and distant relationships.

In the final part of the practice, the wish for happiness extends to all living beings. This further enhances the concept of the interconnected and shared nature of suffering and happiness amongst all living beings. Tibetan Buddhist writings describe that wherever there is space, we can find living beings. All the beings, including simple organisms and animals, are striving for happiness. As we can see in humans, the underlying wish for genuine happiness can go astray and morph into mistaken drives for hedonistic pleasure. Similarly in animals, the fundamental drive for genuine happiness translates due to ignorance mostly into biological needs of survival. Lack of awareness and higher cognitive functioning prevent animals from looking for happiness any further. Nevertheless, from the perspective of Dzogchen, consciousness of all sentient beings contains the element of pure awareness which is their true nature and the ultimate source of genuine happiness.

Importantly, the practice of loving kindness is not only an intellectual exercise. The practice of loving kindness entails an explicit emphasis on the emotional experience. This is more prominent here than in the initial contemplations on happiness at the motivational level of mind training. In the practice of loving kindness, the Dzogchen practitioner is invited to evoke the experiential element of the emotion through visualizations, thoughts and perceptions which enhance the vividness and intensity of the experience.

Connecting with suffering: Compassion

Loving kindness and compassion (karuṇā in both Pāli and Sanskrit) are said to be two sides of the same coin. While loving kindness focuses on the vision of happiness, compassion zooms in on the reality of suffering. When we are faced with suffering, we sometimes close down and find ourselves turning away from the difficulty. We do not want to connect with our own or others' suffering and pain. This avoidance of suffering may arise as a result of overemphasis on pain, sadness and heaviness and as a result compassion can sometimes be misperceived as sadness or grief. When we open our heart and mind to suffering, the experience of compassion can temporarily lead to sadness. But when we generate true compassion, instead of shutting down to suffering, we connect with the difficulty in our lives and focus on the genuine wish for freedom from suffering. After the initial burst of sadness we respond to suffering with genuine compassion which is full of hope. We may notice that compassion actually entails an element of lightness which gives us the power and courage to endure difficulty and help others in the moments of suffering.

Unlike compassion, sadness can lead to depression marked by a lack of energy and a lack of hope for the future.

Similarly to the practice of loving kindness, meditation on compassion towards our own experience builds the foundation for expansion of the circle of compassion towards others. If we cannot connect with our own suffering and develop compassion for ourselves, it is very difficult to cultivate genuine compassion for others. Especially in the Western culture where we often identify with our negative self-beliefs and self-criticism, it is important that we first learn to be a little more gentle, patient, friendly and compassionate with ourselves. Without these qualities of warmth, it would be hard to find the courage to face our afflictive mental habits. Without compassion, we may remain clinging to defense mechanisms of the mistaken notions of who we are in order to protect the image about the self we have created over years and decades.

Just like practices on loving kindness, meditations on compassion involve a progression from compassion for ourselves, to those who are close to us (family and friends), neutral persons, people we have difficulty with and finally all sentient beings. While loving kindness recognizes the shared yearning for happiness of all sentient beings, compassion highlights their shared experience of suffering. When contemplating compassion for our enemies or cruel people in general, we consider the afflictive mental state in which the harmful action originated. Being in that mental state is in itself an experience of severe suffering. In addition, the perpetual conditioning of the mind in the afflictive states and harmful actions will result in further suffering of these people in the future when they experience the consequences of their afflictions. So by wishing those who harm others to be free from suffering, we wish them to be free from the afflictions which cause suffering to them and others.

Aside from the feelings of hope and courage which accompany compassion, there is also an element of readiness to help which arises together with the experience of compassion. When we witness somebody harming another being, we do not remain passive in the experience of compassion. Guided by compassion, we do what is in our power to stop the harmful action. In this way, compassion and a tendency to act wisely become closely intertwined. It is sometimes said that, without wisdom, compassion can be misplaced and blind. This would for example be the case if our compassion for a person prevented us from stopping her from harming herself or others. On the other hand, knowledge separated from compassion can lead to great harm. Looking back at the history and the current situation in the world, we can find many cases where knowledge abused by confused leaders lacking compassion leads to great suffering.

Wars and recent crises of financial systems are good examples of knowledge about technology and finance being detached from compassion and used for ego-centered hedonistic purposes.

Gradients of compassion

We may wonder whether it is possible to experience different levels of intensity and even different kinds of compassion. Tibetan Buddhist teachings of Dzogchen describe three distinct gradients of compassion (Dzogchen Ponlop Rinpoche 2004). The basic notion of compassion arises from the dualistic view of self and others which focuses on the immediate forms of suffering we witness in everyday life. This type of compassion aims to alleviate illness, hunger, lack of shelter, abuse and poverty. It is based on philosophical principles and arises mostly from analysis and reflection. Importantly, just like all other types of compassion, the experience of compassion is generated from genuine unconditional caring for others. It is distinct from pity, which is experienced as a result of shame, guilt or the need to be acknowledged as an altruistic person.

The second gradient of compassion focuses on the nature of phenomena and looks beyond obvious suffering (Dzogchen Ponlop Rinpoche 2004). It recognizes that the immediate forms of suffering are manifestations of deeper origins of suffering in the confused mind. Because of this, the experience of compassion encompasses the wish to be free from immediate suffering such as an illness and also its deeper causes, afflictive emotions in the mind. When this is accomplished the compassionate and wise nature of the mind can fully manifest.

The highest form of compassion which is particularly salient in Dzogchen is described as non-referential (Dzogchen Ponlop Rinpoche 2004). This type of compassion does not involve thinking, contemplation, analysis, visualization or conscious development of the experience of compassion. Rather, the experience of compassion arises naturally and radiates from the mind of the practitioner automatically at the mere sight of a sentient being. This type of compassion is sometimes described as the unconditional love of a mother towards her only child extended to all living beings. Cultivation of non-referential compassion is of great importance in Dzogchen because non-referential compassion is inherent to the ultimate nature of the mind from which it springs without striving. Realization and stabilization of our experience in this deepest unchanging aspect of the mind are the goals of Dzogchen practices.

In general, the description of the gradients of compassion exemplifies why loving kindness and compassion are at the heart of Buddhist practice in Dzogchen. Practices of loving kindness and compassion alone can lead to direct understanding of the ultimate nature of the mind. This is because loving kindness and compassion arise naturally from the purest aspect of our consciousness. In this way, development of loving kindness and compassion is a necessary prerequisite to the practices exploring the nature of our consciousness in Dzogchen.

Neuroscientific evidence on compassion

Only a few studies have so far assessed the effects of loving kindness and compassion on the brain. One study (Lutz et al. 2008b) tested brain responses to emotional sounds – such as a sound of a crying baby – in advanced meditators and meditation novices while they were practicing loving kindness/compassion meditation. The study found increased activation in the insula and anterior cingulate regions of the brain in meditators, which suggests enhanced emotional processing and heightened responsiveness to sounds of distress. This may indicate that meditation on loving kindness and compassion increases the likelihood of turning towards others who are suffering. In addition, there was an increase in activation in the temporoparietal regions which possibly reflects mental activity associated with readiness to help.

In support of neuroplasticity resulting from training in wholesome emotions, another study on loving kindness and compassion showed that with practice these mental states can be induced and sustained at will (Lutz et al. 2004). In this research, advanced Tibetan Buddhist meditators were asked to generate a state of unconditional compassion on and off in blocks lasting one minute. The results showed that the state of non-referential compassion was associated with high-amplitude gamma-frequency oscillations in the brain and this response was clearly distinct for the compassion blocks only. It is too early to say what exactly this finding means in terms of cognitive processing. Gamma oscillations of smaller amplitude are often associated with shifts in conscious awareness. For example, with regard to sensory awareness, gamma oscillations can reflect the moment of binding when we consciously recognize an object such as a table in front of us instead of perceiving it as a disjointed combination of wood and metal (Engel and Singer 2001). In the case of compassion, high-amplitude gamma activity could be associated with a holistic, broadly encompassing, compassionate, non-conceptual state of awareness. Much more research is needed to understand the cognitive and neural correlates of loving kindness and compassion, but it is encouraging to see that explorations of emotions such as compassion are making their way into the mainstream of research (Goetz et al. 2010).

Strengthening positive emotions: Rejoicing

Rejoicing (muditā in both Pāli and Sanskrit) complements loving kindness and compassion through focus on wholesome mental states, events and actions. It counters habitual focus on negative experience, upsetting events, problems that need to be fixed, issues which need to be resolved. With this mindset most of our wholesome experiences simply go unnoticed. Long-term, the habitual focus on difficulty negatively impacts on our mood and stress levels. It can lead to a spiral of negative thoughts, feelings and self-beliefs characterized by increased sensitivity to and memory bias towards negative experience (Hamilton and Gotlib 2008). Rejoicing is a way to balance this negative bias and create an upward spiral of self-perpetuating focus on the positive (Fredrickson and Joiner 2002).

In the practice of rejoicing we purposefully bring to our mind occasions when we experienced or acted out of loving kindness and compassion. We can also recall unconditional kindness that some people have shown us or others. These could be powerful events, for example cases when a disaster brought people together, or just small everyday gestures. It is very useful to spend a few minutes at the end of each day recalling wholesome experiences. We often experience wholesome emotions or act in a whole-some way without noticing. It can be healing to explore the wholesome aspects of our experience for a change. We may find that there are more positive and wholesome occasions, feelings and actions in our lives than we would have thought.

From the Buddhist point of view the practice of rejoicing is closely linked to the teachings on causes and effects of our mental states and actions. Tibetan Buddhist teachings say that the impact of rejoicing is similar to doing the action or having the experience in which we are rejoicing ourselves. Therefore, it is important to rejoice in wholesome activity only. If we rejoice in afflictions, or in harm, the consequences are similar to us doing harm or experiencing afflictive mental states first-hand. Going back to the foundational level of mind training in Dzogchen, wholesomeness of actions, thoughts and emotions is determined by the motivation which drives them. In this way, even small acts arising from unconditional compassion can be more virtuous than great gestures done with the motivation to gain recognition or to appear altruistic in others' eyes.

While the focus is typically on wholesome actions, we can simply rejoice in our and others' well-being, genuine happiness, state of awareness filled with compassion and loving kindness. One of the most useful objects of rejoicing is our own meditation practice and progress in contemplative mind training. This is very useful, especially if we are in a long-term retreat or when we have been meditating regularly for months or years while leading an active life. Long-term practitioners can sometimes slip into a dull routine and continue their practice out of habit without really progressing on the path. Rejoicing in practice can revive our interest in meditation and help us gain new energy and motivation for the contemplative mind training.

In the practice of rejoicing we can start by bringing to our mind somebody who is an embodiment of balance, virtue and well-being for us. For Buddhist practitioners this would often be their teacher. Then we can focus on beneficial selfless actions of others directed at us. In the next step we consider our own wholesome mental states and actions, our meditation practice. Here we need to be cautious not to slip into arrogance which arises when we forget the interdependent nature of our achievements, all those who contributed to our success – our friends, family, supporters, teachers. It is therefore useful to bring to our mind the broader context of our achievements when we rejoice in them. In the final steps of the meditation on rejoicing, we can extend the radius of our practice to include rejoicing in the well-being and selfless actions of people we do not know in person. We may simply remind ourselves that in every moment there are people unconditionally helping others – teachers encouraging their pupils, parents caring for their children, health professionals helping the sick, spiritual teachers broadening the horizons of our awareness.

Rejoicing is an excellent antidote to jealousy. Rather than reacting to others' success in the pursuit of genuine happiness with jealousy, we rejoice in their achievements. From the Buddhist perspective in this way we are sowing the seeds of our own happiness. Interestingly, this traditional approach seems to be to some extent aligned with what we have learned about perspective taking, empathy and observing others' actions in Western psychology and neuroscience. When we are empathizing with others' actions, we engage mental states and brain regions similar to those active in the person performing the actions (Car et al. 2003). The same holds for visual imagery (Slotnick et al. 2012) and also recalling our own and others' thoughts, emotions and actions. This lends support to the proposition that through the practice of rejoicing we train our brain in the actual experience we are rejoicing in.

Broadening the scope: Equanimity

The last of the four wholesome emotions – equanimity – integrates and enhances the development of the other three. Equanimity means that we are able to cultivate loving kindness and compassion equally towards all beings regardless of whether they are friendly or hostile, dull and ignorant or warm-hearted, close to us or not. Equanimity is sometimes confused with indifference – some people believe that not being moved by anything is the meaning of equanimity. But equanimity does not have an emotion-less quality.

In the practice of equanimity (Pāli: upekkhā, Sanskrit: upekṣā), we train in the cultivation of loving kindness and compassion impartially, with a particular focus on feelings of aversion and attachment. We can do this by imagining three people. The first person is somebody we like, somebody close to us. The second person is someone we do not know well and do not have strong positive or negative feelings towards. Finally, the last person is somebody we have difficulty with or it could be a hostile person we may not know personally. In the actual practice we gradually develop loving kindness and compassion for each one of the three people and explore how our emotional experience changes when we move from the person close to us to the neutral person and then the hostile person. Of course, there is extra affection we hold for those who are close to us, but genuine loving kindness and compassion are qualities different from ordinary feelings of affinity and love. They connect with the wish for genuine happiness, for freedom from afflictions and do not contain the implicit fear of loss or change inherent in the ordinary affection. Similarly, we examine the deeper roots of contempt and aversion we may feel towards somebody who harmed us. We invite a broader, wiser perspective on suffering and happiness and include the hostile person in it. In this sense the qualities of loving kindness and compassion combined with equanimity transcend the boundaries of personal, cultural and societal divisions.

In the Mahāyāna tradition the key to cultivation of equanimity is the recognition that all sentient beings without exception desire happiness and want to be free from suffering. It is this shared motivation driving all beings and similarity in their experience which enables us to see beyond the ordinary mental states of like and dislike. In the context of Dzogchen, the practice of equanimity reminds us that the minds of all sentient beings, no matter how confused, contain pristine awareness. This pure aspect of consciousness does not fully manifest because of misguided perceptions of happiness and suffering they hold. In the practice of equanimity we contemplate this deep similarity in the ultimate nature of consciousness amongst all sentient beings and this can broaden our horizons of understanding who we are and how we relate to others.

Practicing the four healthy emotions in everyday life

In Tibetan Buddhism the four healthy emotions are usually practiced in a progression starting with loving kindness, then compassion, followed by rejoicing and equanimity. This particular order is meaningful in the context of cultivation of mental balance. When we practice loving kindness, we sometimes get ungrounded by lofty visions of happiness but compassion brings us back to the reality of suffering. When we are not very skilled at practicing compassion, we can slip into and maintain feelings of sadness and grief. This divergence from the true meaning of compassion is countered by rejoicing – switching the focus to wholesome thoughts, emotions and activities. Finally, we meditate on equanimity to bring the qualities of loving kindness, compassion and rejoicing to the next level, which in Dzogchen builds a link between the cultivation of emotional balance and exploration of the nature of consciousness.

Even though we have so far mostly discussed the development of the four healthy emotions 'on the cushion' it can be very inspiring to train in these wholesome qualities of mind in everyday situations. Each day we can cultivate wholesome habits of responding to whatever we encounter with one of the four healthy emotions. If we see somebody yearning for happiness and perhaps looking for it in the wrong places, we develop loving kindness for them and we wish them to find genuine sources of happiness. If we witness suffering, we let compassion arise naturally and examine ways to respond to difficulty in wise and useful ways. If we witness selfless acts of kindness, we rejoice in them. Whatever arises in our mind, we respond with the four healthy emotions instead of our usual indifferent, cynical, arrogant, or angry reactions.

In this way, we can try to practice the four healthy emotions while having a conversation with a frustrated colleague at work, while waiting in line at a supermarket, when we are stuck in a traffic jam or when we receive good news about our friend's success. If we turn the focus towards our own experience, we can respond with loving kindness and compassion whenever we slip into a cycle of excessive self-criticism and anxiety. Just recognizing the difficulty we are facing and approaching our experience from a gentle, forgiving, and spacious perspective may provide the courage and wisdom we need to move forward. Whatever the circumstances, favorable or not, we can skillfully practice the four healthy emotions and in that way transform our mind step by step every day hundreds of times. In this way, we gradually condition our mind and brain in emotional balance.

Scientific evidence supporting the outlined complementary progression of training in healthy emotions is virtually absent. It would be intriguing to examine the impact of the four healthy emotions cultivated separately and together. It would also be interesting to explore how mind training in the four healthy emotions could be tailored to individual needs of practitioners. In the Tibetan Buddhist tradition, teachers often recommend their students to focus on one practice or another based on their mental propensities. Outside the Buddhist context, a similar approach may find its place in therapeutic and preventive practice.

Bodhicitta: The bridge from emotional balance to enlightenment

The core purpose of cultivating the four wholesome emotions is in the Mahāyāna tradition the development of boddhicitta – a quality of mind which from the perspective of Dzogchen bridges the third and fourth level of the mind training pyramid. In this context, boddhicitta brings together cultivation of emotional balance with the exploration of different levels of consciousness, and ultimately, the pristine awareness of our mind. In Tibetan Buddhism, boddhicitta is divided into relative and absolute (Patrul Rinpoche 1998). Relative bodhicitta is the mental state of genuine heartfelt aspiration to attain enlightenment and help all sentient beings achieve it combined with the actual steps we take to achieve this goal. The powerful wish to attain enlightenment is singled out as the intention aspect of relative bodhicitta (Santideva 1997). When this aspiration translates into practice and motivates us to engage in meditation practice which will lead to enlightenment, we develop the application aspect of relative bodhicitta (Santideva 1997).

It is sometimes easy to reduce relative bodhicitta into a simplistic and superficial wish for everybody to be happy without really understanding or connecting with what enlightenment means. Relative bodhicitta goes much deeper and integrates components of logical analysis, emotional experience and action tendency. In the tradition of Dzogchen, the logical analysis component means that bodhicitta is born from extensive and deep consideration of the sources of our happiness, from understanding that ultimately there is no freedom from suffering until we abide in the pristine awareness of our mind. The emotional experience of relative bodhicitta manifests itself as a clear, intense yearning for ourselves and others to be free from afflictions of the mind forever. It fills our whole mind with warmth and strong motivation to engage in mind training which helps us realize the pristine nature of our mind. This emotional tone stays with us continuously and helps us transform ordinary activity into mind training for enlightenment. Finally, the application aspect of relative bodhicitta represents the action tendency arising from the contemplation and emotional experience of bodhicitta. We not only stay with the wish for enlightenment, but actively engage in mind training at the final level of the pyramid.

In contrast to relative bodhicitta, the absolute bodhicitta in Dzogchen shifts the focus of mind training from practices leading to the recognition of the ultimate nature of the mind to the actual experience of the pristine aspect of our awareness. Here absolute bodhicitta is the state of recognizing the nature of the mind and stabilizing our consciousness in this pure mental state. It is the fulfillment of relative bodhicitta and culmination of our mind training. As such, absolute bodhicitta is no different from enlightenment itself.

Practice: The four wholesome emotions

As always at the beginning of your practice, you start by settling your body in a comfortable but alert position. You may want to scan your body for tension and gradually relax any tense muscle groups. Then you balance your autonomous nervous system by five deep in-breaths and out-breaths, with the out-breath being longer than the in-breath. Now you can spend a few minutes developing the intention for your practice and, if you like, follow this by a brief calm-abiding practice where you gently focus on your breath. You may want to go back to the practice sections in previous chapters if you need to refresh your memories of any of the meditations we have discussed previously.

Loving kindness

Now we can start with the practice of the four healthy emotions, developing loving kindness first. If you are doing these practices as part of your daily meditation sequence, you may want to spend a minute or two at each step of the practice. Or maybe you decide to spend more time on some aspects of the meditations and less on others. If you are practicing in retreat and make the practices on the four wholesome emotions the focus of your mind training, you could easily dedicate hours to these contemplations.

You may want to begin by creating an image of a small child in your mind. When you see the image with enough clarity, you may like to shift your focus on to the emotional experience this visualization is eliciting in your mind. You may try to connect with the emotion and let it develop. Perhaps you notice a feeling of warmth which can be described as a wish for the child to be genuinely happy.

Now you can extend this feeling to yourself, wishing for yourself to be happy. Maybe you find it useful to remind yourself that what we mean by happiness here is the mental balance of intention, attention, emotions and actions. You may want to start developing a vision of genuine happiness for yourself. What are your aspirations of genuine happiness? What would it be like to bring them to fruition?

In the next step you extend this feeling to those who are close to you – your family and your closest friends. May they be happy in the genuine sense.

Then you try to expand the focus of your meditation by including people you are neutral to in your meditation. Those might be persons you see in a supermarket, people who pass by when you are walking down the street. Wish them to be genuinely happy as well.

You may now try to broaden your perspective even further and extend the feeling of happiness to those we have difficulty with – people who you find challenging to be with, even people who harmed you or are harming others. Remind yourself that they are acting out of ignorance and unhappiness and, if they were genuinely happy, they would not harm others.

Finally, you can extend the wish for happiness to all sentient beings without exception. You may recognize that wherever there is life, there is yearning for happiness.

Compassion

Compassion is the genuine wish for yourself and all sentient beings to be free from suffering and its causes. This means being free from the afflictions of craving, ignorance, anger, jealousy, arrogance, and their derivatives. You may want to bring to your mind that compassion is not the same as sadness and includes qualities of lightness, courage and hope. This may help you to recognize any divergence into sadness and grief in your practice, and help you bring your focus back on to compassion.

You may begin by imagining somebody who is close to you and is going through some difficulty. Try to visualize this clearly and, if you feel comfortable, connect with the feeling the image elicits in your mind. Explore the emotion that arises. It can perhaps be described as a powerful yearning that the difficulty would pass. You may even have an intense feeling or wish to do anything possible to help, to free them from the suffering they are experiencing.

Now you may try to extend this feeling to yourself, recognizing and connecting with your own suffering and wishing yourself to be free from it. May this difficulty pass, may I be free from suffering.

In the next step you may extend this feeling to all those who are close to you. Let it be more than a thought; if it feels right, you may try to connect with the emotional experience and let it develop.

Now extend this emotion to those you are neutral to, recognizing that even though you do not know them closely, they are also deeply familiar with the experience of suffering. You may explore what it is like to wish them to be free from their suffering.

The next step can be difficult. Here we bring to our mind those we have difficulty with, those we have disagreements with, people who harmed us. If you feel comfortable proceeding, try to develop compassion for them as well, recognizing that the mental state they are in when they are harming others is very painful. You may also recognize that their negative actions will lead to negative consequences in the future. May they be free from suffering of the afflictions as well and not cause suffering to themselves and others.

Finally, extend the feeling of genuine compassion to all sentient beings.

Rejoicing

Now we shift our focus on to wholesome thoughts, emotions and actions. You can start by bringing to your mind something people who are close to you have done for you. You may recall the kindness of your parents or work with something as simple as remembering a cup of tea your friend or partner made for you today. Bring these joyous events to your mind and stay with the emotional experience this elicits in you.

In the next step you can rejoice in wholesome things you have done for yourself and others, be they big acts of kindness or just small gestures, intentions or thoughts. Can you think of something wholesome you have done today or yesterday? How did it make you feel?

You can now try to rejoice in wholesome actions of people you do not know personally and don't have strong positive or negative feelings towards. Maybe you can think of a stranger kindly smiling at you or somebody giving way to you in busy traffic. What emotional experience arises in your mind when you think about these events? Can you think of an act of kindness you have done for other people you do not know in person? How did it feel?

Finally, you may explore expanding the practice of rejoicing to include wholesome thoughts, emotions, and actions without specific distinction. You may simply recognize that in every moment there are some beings selflessly benefiting others.

Equanimity

The practice of equanimity develops our ability to cultivate loving kindness, compassion and rejoicing impartially, transcending the biased distinctions between those who are close to us and those who are not.

You can start the meditation on equanimity by bringing to your mind three people – one of them being a person close to you, the second being a person you don't have strong feelings for or against and the last one being a hostile person. Now try to develop loving kindness towards the person you are close to, then extend the feeling to the neutral person and finally the hostile person. As you proceed from one person to the next, you may explore changes in your emotional experience and thoughts. How is your feeling of loving kindness for the hostile person different from loving kindness for the person who is close to you?

Now you may want to go through the same sequence but practice compassion. Bring the three people to your mind and gradually develop compassion for each one of them.

Are the quality and intensity of compassion for the person you are close to the same as the quality of compassion for the neutral person? If you set aside the extra affection you hold for the person you are close to, do you find any difference between the compassion you feel for the close person and the hostile person?

Summary: Chapter 4

When some stability and pliancy of attention has been achieved, we can work more closely with emotion-related aspects of our mind. Scientific theories of emotions describe emotional experience, emotion-specific thoughts, physiological reactions of the body and tendencies to act as distinct components of emotions. Western research on emotions focuses on two main aspects: valence measured on a scale from pleasant to unpleasant and intensity of emotions. In contrast, Buddhist psychology does not recognize emotions as a separate category; rather, it discusses mental states similar to emotions based on their wholesomeness – well-being-promoting or harmful effects. According to this system, wholesome emotions such as friendliness and compassion are associated with well-being. Afflictive emotions, for example anger, greed and arrogance, interfere with well-being.

Basic contemplative training in the cultivation of wholesome emotions proceeds from loving kindness and compassion to rejoicing and equanimity. Loving kindness develops a vision of genuine happiness for us and others. Compassion develops the courage to see clearly obvious and subtle forms of suffering together with their deeper causes. It results in a sincere wish to train on the path that ends suffering and to support others in their quest to be free from suffering. Rejoicing balances compassion through focus on wholesome thoughts, emotions and actions we and others engage in every day, often without noticing. It fuels our determination to progress further in the mind training. Finally, equanimity teaches how to extend the highest degree of loving kindness and compassion to everybody – including those people we do not know, even hostile people, and in the end all sentient beings. This can help us discover the deeper meaning of happiness and suffering linked to the interconnectedness and shared nature of human experience. Somewhat paradoxically, the willingness to connect with suffering and see its causes with clarity leads to a deeper experience of well-being and happiness, and also opens the door to exploration of the ultimate nature of our mind.

Science only begins to understand the beneficial effects of wholesome emotions on our body, mind and brain. Initial research demonstrates high levels of neural plasticity in training of compassion. It also shows that it is possible to induce compassion at will. Specifically, research with highly skilled Tibetan Buddhist meditators indicates that the experience of compassion is associated with distinct patterns of brain oscillations which are unique to this meditation practice. Other findings show that meditators react to emotional sounds of distress with heightened activation in the brain regions associated with emotion processing such as the anterior cingulate and also other regions, possibly reflecting readiness to help.

Chapter 5

Exploring consciousness

Science and Buddhism: Consciousness as the key topic of science

Consciousness is perhaps the most intriguing topic in philosophy and science – central to our understanding of human existence. Yet, for most of the history of modern science, consciousness has been considered to be outside the arena of phenomena which can be examined by scientific tools. It was only at the beginning of the 20th century that the discipline of psychology turned its attention on to consciousness and made it its primary subject of inquiry (Titchener 1912). In these early conceptions, consciousness was equated with the awareness of our sensations, feelings, perceptions and thoughts. This approach focused on the subjective, experiential aspect of consciousness. The main research method used in investigation of consciousness was introspection based on observations of mental processes in our own mind. For example, research participants could be asked to look at differently colored shapes and rate the intensity and quality of their experience. But despite careful considerations about potential shortcomings of this method (Titchener 1912), the introspection-based research on consciousness did not prove very fruitful. This was mainly because results of experiments which used introspection differed vastly across research laboratories – components of perception and thinking discovered through introspection varied from one school to another, depending on their assumptions and schemas applied to the classification and interpretation of conscious experience.

The lack of replicability of introspection-based research led John Watson (1913) to formulate a proposal which would shift the paradigm focus in psychology from the mind to observable behavior. Watson even suggested that psychology as a scientific discipline should completely eliminate from its vocabulary terms such as consciousness, mental states, thoughts and imagery. He said: 'The time seems to have come when psychology must discard all reference to consciousness; when it need no longer delude itself into thinking that it is making mental states the object of observation' (Watson 1913: 163). After this sweeping criticism of introspectionism, the behaviorist approach dominated the field of psychology for more than 40 years. However, after several decades of behaviorist research it became apparent that this approach is not able to address questions about fundamental aspects of the human mind such as thinking and imagery. We can, for example, easily recall a happy episode from our childhood or visualize in our mind the layout of our bedroom, yet from the behaviorist point of view everyday mental processes such as these could not be studied by psychology.

Surprisingly, the main demonstration of how limiting the behaviorist approach was did not come from research on thinking, but from arguments about sentence construction in language. In 1959 Noam Chomsky proposed the theory of grammar which argued that sentence composition across languages is governed by a set of algorithm-like rules (Chomsky 1959a, 1959b). Behaviorism could not explain the processes in the mind which could underlie such operations since mental states were more or less a taboo in their paradigm. Chomsky's account suggested that, if at least some mental processes have algorithmic nature, they could be likened to operations of a computer. The computer analogy provided a framework for research and development of models explaining processes of the mind. This proposal started another shift in the methods and phenomena of inquiry in psychology – this time towards mental states and processes neglected by behaviorists commonly summed up under the label of cognition, involving perception, thought, language, decision making and emotions. Cognitivist theories work with mental representations and computations, and use experimental methods mostly relying on research participants' reaction times to carefully selected combinations of stimuli to develop models of cognitive mechanisms underlying mental functioning. This approach is still prevalent in the current experimental psychology.

Despite this revival of the study of mind in the discipline of psychology, the notion of consciousness remained mostly untouched by science until the 1990s. One of the main impulses for the return of the topic of consciousness into the realm of scientific inquiry was work by a philosopher David Chalmers (1995), who divided questions about consciousness into 'easy' ones and the 'hard problem'. Chalmers argued that easy questions about consciousness could be addressed using methods of cognitive sciences which include – amongst other sciences –

neuroscience, psychology and computational science. These branches of science provide the tools, for example, for the study of biological brain wave markers of consciousness linked to vigilance and cognitive arousal in differential states of sleep, being awake or in coma.

Neuroscience of consciousness and the enigma of conscious experience

Over the last decade neuroscience provided novel insights into the neural underpinnings of consciousness. Some of the most interesting findings relate to the role of synchronous neural firing in conscious perceptual experience. Specifically, it has been found (Engel and Singer 2001) that conscious recognition of an object is associated with synchronous firing of neural assemblies in the gamma-band range (brain wave frequency above 20 Hz). Another intriguing line of investigation using magnetic resonance imaging described a default mode network (DMN) – a network of brain areas which are active when people are simply asked to rest with their eyes closed or focused on a fixation point (Raichle et al. 2001). Since the brain is always active, even when we are resting, it is possible to derive levels of interconnectedness in activation across brain regions in a resting state. With regard to investigation of consciousness, research shows that the degree of DMN activity relates to the levels of consciousness in patients who are not able to communicate as a result of brain damage. One research study (Vanhaudenhuyse et al. 2010) compared DMN activation in healthy controls, coma patients, patients with minimal levels of consciousness and those with locked-in syndrome (conscious but overtly unresponsive). The findings showed no differences between healthy controls and patients with locked-in syndrome but there was significantly less activity in DMN in minimally conscious patients and even less in coma patients. In addition, the study reported stronger connectivity of precuneus – brain structure implicated in conscious experience (Cavanna and Trimble 2006) – in minimally conscious patients in comparison to patients in coma.

In contrast to these 'easy' questions about neural underpinnings of consciousness, the hard problem of consciousness cannot be readily tackled using similar scientific methods. The hard problem is about the conscious experience, the phenomenological element of consciousness (Chalmers 1995). The difficulty arises due to the subjective, unique and private nature of conscious experience. Even in cases of simple perceptual experience – for example, when we are looking at the sky with a friend – it is impossible to compare the actual experience of blue color across the two minds. There is no way to measure directly whether the experience – the 'what it feels like' element of consciousness (Nagel 1974) – elicited by exactly the same sensory input produces identical conscious experiences.

Certainly, using methods of neuroscience we could measure activation in the visual and emotional areas of the brain, but this is where the difficulty arises in its full power. If we measure brain activity induced by looking at the sky we are collecting so-called 'third-person' data which are quantifiable and replicable across researchers if they use exactly the same methods and procedures. For some researchers, the neuroscientific data would present a way to explain the conscious experience; for others these would be mere correlates detached from the experience as such. A thought experiment suggested by Jackson (1982) might be helpful to demonstrate the point here. Imagine a neuroscientist who has extensive knowledge about brain activation in color perception. The neuroscientist knows exactly how the wavelength of red color impacts on the retina and induces neural impulses which are transferred via the optical nerve to the lateral geniculate nucleus (a structure in the thalamus of the brain) then primary visual cortex and higher visual areas of the brain. However, the neuroscientist is actually blind and, despite all this knowledge, has never experienced red color. In other words, the experiential element of red color is missing in the neuroscientist's understanding of red color. This indicates that there is more to explaining human experience than the mere knowledge acquired using third-person methods.

So how can we investigate the conscious experience itself? Perhaps we need to invite introspective methods back into the realm of science, despite their bad reputation from the early days of psychology (Chalmers 2004; Nielsen and Kaszniak 2007). Introspection seems to be the best tool for exploration of private conscious experience – only the individuals having the conscious experience can provide us with information regarding 'what it feels like' for them to have that experience. Still, there are many potential shortcomings associated with the use of introspection. Most worrisome is the fact that conscious experience can be modified by other cognitive processes and changes in attentional focus (Frijda 2001b; Schooler 2002). The act of reporting about a conscious experience often causes a shift in attention in the direction of the report and away from the experience itself, which can lead to a decrease in intensity and possible change in quality of the experience. Moreover, use of specific reporting schemes such as scales imposes a prescribed framework on the report of conscious experience and this can reshape the nature of the original experience. As noted by Nielsen and Kaszniak (2007), the use of open-ended reports is also problematic because different people can spontaneously attend to different aspects of their conscious experience and that diminishes our ability to compare reports across research participants. Overall, it seems that we cannot avoid most of these problems in the research on conscious experience. This is where the Buddhist approaches to investigation of consciousness based on introspection can provide some novel insights.

Buddhist approaches to introspection

Interestingly, Buddhist psychology and Buddhist systems of teaching and practice have been developed almost exclusively using the method of introspection. This may seem hardly possible if we consider the early failures and many imperfections of introspection documented in the history of Western psychology. We could easily conclude that, because of the private nature of conscious experience, the assessment of conscious experience from the perspective of the person having the experience is unique and non-replicable or generalizable across people. This is where an important difference between Buddhist and Western psychological approaches based on introspection steps in. The Buddhist tradition clearly recognizes that refined and stabilized attention is the necessary prerequisite for reliable observation of mental processes using introspection (Varela et al. 1991; Wallace 2006). Applying the tool of refined attentional abilities, meditators across Buddhist traditions and geographical regions have been, over more than 25 centuries, arriving at similar accounts of the mind. How could stability of attention assure such replicability and reliability of introspection?

A possible explanation can be elucidated by some of the distinctions about conscious experience made by modern cognitive science. It has been suggested that the category of conscious experience can be divided into two subcategories – conscious and meta-conscious mental activity (Schooler 2002). Mind wandering can be a good example to demonstrate the difference (Schooler 2002). All of us have from time to time the experience of diverging into thoughts irrelevant to the topic of a conversation we are having with somebody. When we notice this we bring our attention back to the conversation. During the moment of mind wandering we were having a conscious experience of the irrelevant thoughts, but not the knowledge that we are mind wandering – meta-consciousness of the experience (Schooler 2002). A similar distinction has been drawn in the context of research into emotional experience where some researchers differentiate between raw phenomenality and reflective consciousness (Lane 2000; Nielsen and Kaszniak 2007). Raw phenomenality includes basic experience of changes in different components of emotion without thoughts about those changes whereas reflective consciousness is a mix of these basic feelings and cognitive evaluation and labeling.

The meta-conscious mental activity is essential to introspection, but is subject to two main shortcomings which can produce inaccuracy in our meta-conscious representations of experience (Schooler 2002). The first shortcoming relates to the distance in time from the experience we apply meta-consciousness to. If we reflect on an experience which is more distant in time – in terms of minutes, hours, days and months – we are more likely to misrepresent it and impose our own schemas on to the original experience. The second potential source of inaccuracy is when we are trying to 'translate' the original experience during the process of meta-consciousness into another mode (Schooler 2002). For example, we may want to report about our experience of smelling a rose using words. This 'translation' of information from the domain of non-verbal conscious experience into words can arguably modify the original experience based on our schemas and limitations of verbal reports. We may, for instance, start imposing frameworks of gradients and qualities of smells, pleasantness and unpleasantness on to the original experience and in this way morph it slightly into the shape of the verbal descriptions.

Coming back to Buddhist introspective methods, stability and enhanced ability to monitor attention – the skills of mindfulness and meta-awareness – seem to reduce the two sources of introspective error significantly. When it comes to the temporal distance between conscious experience and meta-consciousness, well-trained meta-awareness may enable the meditator to switch to the meta-consciousness mode with a minimal temporal gap. In other words, it takes meditators very little time to notice that their mind is experiencing frustration or that their stream of thinking just wandered into irrelevant thoughts. In this way, the meditator greatly increases the frequency of meta-conscious moments and their accuracy. In addition, mindfulness – the stability of attention – enables the practitioner to stay in the raw phenomenality or meta-conscious modes for longer without necessarily imposing verbal or other schemas on to the raw experience. In this way, the enhanced accuracy and reliability of introspective observation allow for repeated patterns of mental activity to emerge more clearly for each observer and similarity in observations across observers can lead to generalizable convergent views of the mind and consciousness. In the Buddhist context, these refined introspective skills are powerful tools in examining how consciousness works and how it relates to well-being and human potential.

While mostly relying on introspective methodology, Buddhist exploration of consciousness – particularly in the Tibetan Buddhist tradition of Dzogchen – also builds on so-called 'second-person' expertise of an experienced teacher. In this case a teacher uses extensive personal experience in meditation in the assessment and support of adepts on the path. This method is described as 'second-person' because it is based on knowledge gathered through personal introspective observation, but its application extends beyond a personal understanding of the mind into a tailored approach of teaching others. Convergence in knowledge about the mind between a student's introspective observations and expert assessment of a student's progress by the teacher is a further indicator of accuracy and reliability of the findings in the meditative exploration of the mind.

The three layers of consciousness

Based on the investigation of the mind using introspection grounded in enhanced skills of mindfulness and meta-cognition, the Dzogchen tradition distinguishes three main layers of consciousness. The first layer is the ordinary mind we rely on during most of our daily activities. It includes the sensations, perceptions, thoughts, memories and affect we are usually experiencing and can mostly become meta-conscious of if we direct our attention towards the mind. These mental processes enable us to learn new skills, make decisions, and function efficiently in everyday life. This is the aspect of mental processing psychologists and neuroscientists study using questionnaires, reaction time tasks, psychophysiological and neuroimaging methods.

However, as noted at some points in the history of psychology, the ordinary level of conscious experience is only the tip of the iceberg when it comes to the range of mental processes in our mind. For example, in the psychoanalytic tradition of Freud and his followers, a distinction has been drawn between conscious and unconscious processes of the mind. For the most part, we do not have access to the unconscious mind in the regular awake state, but the unconscious processes strongly influence the ways we think and behave overtly. The unconscious aspects of mind can manifest themselves in dreams and become accessible in hypnosis where they can be explored further for therapeutic reasons.

Even though different in purpose and underlying theory from the psychoanalytic approach, the notion of the 'unconscious' mind which influences our conscious experience without our knowledge is also supported by research in current cognitive psychology. For example, it has been shown that words presented on a computer screen very fast (typically for less than 40 ms) and masked by rows of random signs before and after they appear are not consciously noticed by research participants. Nevertheless, they may influence participants' decision making. To demonstrate this, research participants can be asked to make decisions about words on the screen such as whether they are names of farm animals. For example, a word 'cat' can be presented on a computer screen and participants would respond 'yes' in this case. Interestingly, presentation of another word such as 'dog' for less than 40 ms and in a masked format before the word 'cat' appears on the screen speeds up the response to the word 'cat' (Forster 2004). In other words, participants are faster in their decisions about the word 'cat' when it is preceded by the unconsciously perceived priming word 'dog' in comparison to no prime or an unrelated priming word (such as 'rock'). Laboratory studies such as this one demonstrate that unconscious information can indeed impact on our decisions and behavior.

Dzogchen descriptions of the mind beyond the ordinary consciousness also embrace the notion of the unconscious, but approach it from a different perspective. The second layer of consciousness (Sanskrit: ālayavijñāna; Tibetan: kun gzhi nams shes; Ricard 2003; Wallace 2006) described in this tradition is sometimes called the 'substrate consciousness'. It is mostly hidden from our awareness unless we refine our attention abilities of mindfulness and introspection, and also settle the ordinary mind through practices cultivating emotional balance. The stability and vigilance of attention coupled with emotional balance are needed because of the overabundance of mental activity at the ordinary level of consciousness. This 'mental noise' does not allow us to see through the superficial layer of perceptions, thoughts, mental schemas and defensive habits. Once the ordinary level of the mind settles to the point where random impulsive mental activity arises in our practice only occasionally, we are able to apply the introspective observation skills in the examination of substrate consciousness. This layer of consciousness contains more subtle tendencies of behavior, mental habits and temper which influence the ordinary mind. It can determine our inclinations towards certain activities, places and people. It contains the roots of mental frameworks which underlie our construed notions of who we are, our concepts of 'self' or 'I'. In the context of Dzogchen, this layer of consciousness connects with the belief in reincarnation and therefore substrate consciousness is sometimes described as reflecting our tendencies developed over many lifetimes.

The distinctions between the ordinary consciousness and the substrate consciousness are not simply drawn in terms of the conscious versus the unconscious. Most of the descriptions of unconscious processing in experimental psychology and psychoanalysis would, from the Dzogchen point of view, perhaps still fall under the label of the ordinary mind. The training in attentional and emotional balance shifts our ability of perceiving processes of our mind from the ordinary mind to the substrate consciousness – as we calm down the ordinary level of our consciousness, we are able to observe increasingly more aspects of the substrate consciousness. This may lead to new pleasant and unpleasant experiences as we may be faced with memories, impressions, emotions and perceptions long forgotten or suppressed. In some advanced practices of Dzogchen, we let these experiences arise on purpose and observe them fading away into the substrate consciousness. We may even explore their underlying nature. In this way we settle and stabilize our mind at a deeper level. Once some balance at the level of substrate consciousness has been achieved, experiences of bliss, non-conceptuality and luminosity may arise. These are the marks of experiencing the ground state of substrate of consciousness from which our ordinary experiences manifest (Wallace 2006).

However, the substrate consciousness is not the final goal of Dzogchen practices and it is important not to mistake the experiences of non-conceptuality and bliss arising at the level of substrate consciousness with the final, deepest level of our consciousness. From the perspective of Dzogchen, the core of our mind is the pristine awareness (Sanskrit: vidyā; Tibetan: rigpa) which is often described as the experiential recognition of our Buddha nature. It is the pure aspect of our consciousness which is always present, even when we are completely consumed by the chaos of the ordinary mind. No matter how confused or unsettled the mind is, pristine awareness is not modified by the turmoil at the other two levels of consciousness. The final goal of Dzogchen practices is simply to recognize and sustain our consciousness at this ever-present level of ultimate mental balance.

In order to recognize experientially pristine awareness, we need to examine the nature of our conscious experience beyond the substrate consciousness. This is where introspective accounts of conscious experience in words reach their limits. The recognition of pristine awareness is beyond descriptions as our mind reveals new non-conceptual luminous and blissful modes of knowledge and compassion. Nevertheless, from the perspective of practice progression it is useful to discuss some pointers to experiential differences between substrate consciousness and pristine awareness. The first one is that the qualities of non-conceptuality, luminosity and bliss are impossible to separate as they arise in pristine awareness, whereas at the level of substrate consciousness they are separable. Another aspect relates to the individual versus all-encompassing nature of consciousness. While the substrate consciousness is specific to each individual, pristine awareness reaches beyond the individual. This aspect of difference is inherently intertwined with the presence of a subtle notion of an 'I' in the substrate consciousness, while the pristine awareness surpasses the notions of 'I' and 'self' completely. At the heart of the differences is the breakdown of the distinctions between the observer and the observed in the experience of pristine awareness which is not present at any other layer of consciousness. In this way, pristine awareness dissolves many of the limitations of first-person, second-person and third-person methods of investigating the mind since these methods are formulated from the perspective of duality between the observer and the observed. In Dzogchen pristine awareness is considered to be the ultimate source of knowledge about our mind and also outer phenomena.

From the experiential point of view, abiding in pristine awareness purifies our afflictions completely as this level of awareness is not disturbed the by arising of thoughts, emotions and perceptions. These are recognized as manifestations of the nature of the mind without being intertwined with the afflictions of like and dislike, craving, anger, arrogance and ignorance. In contrast, experiences of the substrate consciousness are linked to the stabilized focused states of mind at higher stages of shamatha and as a result they are disturbed by mental activity of thoughts, perceptions and mental images. It is important to keep in mind that the practice of shamatha in itself does not lead to the recognition of pristine awareness. Experience of pristine awareness arises as a result of practices inquiring about the nature of our mind and phenomena around us. In these practices we typically settle the mind in a calm state with little distractions and then watch as thoughts, perceptions and emotions arise and fade away. We explore the source of the mental activity and its characteristics (Pāli: vipassana; Sanskrit: vipasyana; Tibetan: lhaktong). In this way we learn about the nature of mental phenomena and in Dzogchen we also examine the nature of the observer as such. Importantly, the further we go, the less this process of inquiry relies on intellectual reasoning – experiential, non-conceptual modes of knowledge become more prominent instead.

The eight types of consciousness

Aside from the three layers of consciousness, Buddhist Dzogchen texts elucidate further subdivisions of the ordinary consciousness and substrate consciousness. These teachings are mostly based on the work of Mipham Rinpoche called *Gateway to Knowledge* (1997), which was written at the end of the 19th century. The eight types of consciousness include five types of consciousness which roughly correspond to the five senses, the mind consciousness, afflictive consciousness and substrate consciousness.

The first five types of consciousness are eye consciousness, ear consciousness, nose consciousness, tongue consciousness, and body consciousness. These types of consciousness create perceptions of the five senses when a certain type of consciousness meets an external stimulus it is sensitive to through the corresponding sense faculty. For example, a visual image we perceive is only created when the energy the eye is sensitive to meets the eye faculty abiding in our eye and combines with eye consciousness. Similarly for the other four types of consciousness associated with the remaining sense faculties. Importantly, these types of consciousness give rise to perceptions without conceptual association and evaluation. These perceptions only arise in dependence on an object of perception being present, such as a visual image or a sound – the five types of sensory consciousness are not active during imagination or thought when we create mental activity without corresponding input from the outside world.

In contrast, the sixth type of consciousness, which is the mind consciousness, involves thinking. This type of consciousness is not bound to sensations and perceptions immediately available to the first five types of consciousness. The mind consciousness is the building ground of afflictions such as attachment and anger which arise from ignorant ways of thinking. At the same time, the mind consciousness is the core tool of Buddhist mind training because most meditation practices rely heavily on this type of consciousness. The mental faculties of mindfulness and meta-awareness which are the main pillars of attention training arise at the level of mind consciousness. Similarly, practices involving contemplations on happiness, cultivation of the four healthy emotions, as well as visualization practices all employ the mind consciousness. We also work closely with this type of consciousness when we learn to guide our mental activity away from automatic afflictive thought patterns and train in well-being-promoting ways of thinking.

The central role of mind consciousness in meditation derives from its involvement in the three main activities of Buddhist mind training. These are learning about Buddhist teachings, reflecting on the teachings and experiential practice in which we realize the teachings. To illustrate this progression, Buddhist teachers use various metaphors – in one of them they compare the progression of mind training to a glass of water. First, we can be shown a glass of water and told that the water in the glass can quench our thirst. In the second step we consider this more closely, wonder how the water may taste and decide to drink the water when we get thirsty. In the last step we actually drink the water from the glass and experience first-hand what the water tastes like and what it does for our body. Similarly, we learn about mind training, contemplate some aspects of the teachings and then put the instructions into experiential practice. All these steps of Buddhist mind training engage the mind consciousness.

The first six types of consciousness are considered unstable because they arise and vanish at the level of ordinary consciousness. But as a result of their temporary appearances, they are more obviously recognizable than the remaining two types of consciousness, which are called 'stable' because they are continuously present until we achieve enlightenment. These are the afflictive consciousness and the substrate consciousness. The afflictive consciousness is the foundation of our afflictions – a subtle form of attachment to an independent self arises from this source. This clinging on to an 'I' or 'self' in the afflictive consciousness serves as a basis for the mind consciousness which builds up the coarse grasping at a notion of 'self' and this in turn produces the afflictions of craving, anger, and ignorance in the form of negative thoughts and affect. The presence of the afflictive consciousness varies as we progress in our practice based on our ability to abide in pristine awareness. The vast majority of people continuously function on the ordinary level of consciousness and the afflictive consciousness stays present all the time. In practitioners who are able to abide in the pristine awareness in their meditation, the afflictive consciousness is temporarily suspended while meditating but outside of meditation the afflictive consciousness appears again. The afflictive consciousness ceases to exist in practitioners who completely realize the non-existence of self and sustain this realization within and outside meditation. In the Mahāyāna tradition, where 11 levels of accomplishment (Sanskrit: Bhūmis; Tibetan: byang chub sems dpai sa) on the path to complete enlightenment are described, the afflictive consciousness is abandoned at the eighth level and past that level it no longer exists.

The eighth type of consciousness is the substrate consciousness which we have discussed as part of the conception of three levels of consciousness. In the context of the eight types of consciousness, substrate consciousness serves as a basis for all the other seven types of consciousness as they arise from this base. The substrate consciousness is sometimes described in terms of two functions – storage and retrieval of subtle imprints of mental and behavioral tendencies. The first function collects and stores overall patterns of mental functioning and behavior we accumulate over years, decades and, from the perspective of Dzogchen, even lifetimes. The second function enables the stored imprints to reappear again and guide our behavior. The substrate consciousness is involved in practices of attentional and emotional balance when we explore deeper roots of our mental and behavioral tendencies. It is also strongly employed in visualization meditation – it stores and retrieves the visualized sacred images. In these practices through visualization we are able to modify the subtle tendencies accumulated in the substrate consciousness.

The default mode network of the brain and meditation

Whether the differences between levels and types of consciousness can be associated with distinguishable brain correlates is currently an open question. This is where the attempts to reduce or translate states of the mind or consciousness into measurable brain changes may be reaching their limits. Since the distinctions between the levels and types of consciousness in Dzogchen are based on introspective methods tapping into conscious experience, the study of levels and types of consciousness raises questions which are closer to the hard problem of consciousness than to the easy questions about consciousness. From a different angle, it raises questions about the possibility of science which would successfully combine first- and third-person methods in the exploration of consciousness. This will require careful consideration of bridging principles between first-person and third-person accounts – ways to couple introspective observations with neuroscientific data (Chalmers 2004). One of the first tasks in this process will be selection of neural markers which are most likely to detect the changes in consciousness described from the introspective experiential perspective of meditators. Given what we know at this stage about brain function and consciousness, the most likely candidates for such markers are modifications of the oscillatory synchrony of neural firing between different brain regions measured using electroencephalography and differential 'default mode' of brain function – typical state of connectivity between brain regions – assessed using magnetic resonance imaging.

While there are no studies which directly assessed the differences in consciousness outlined in Dzogchen, there is tentative evidence that the default mode of brain function is sensitive to some differences in brain connectivity associated with meditation practice. One study (Brewer et al. 2011) compared activation in the DMN between meditators engaging in three different types of meditation practice and control participants without meditation training. The researchers hypothesized that meditators would show less activation in the DMN because of its association with self-referential modes of processing and random mental activity. The findings confirmed this prediction and the brain activations were consistent across the three types of meditation practice. Additional analysis also indicated increased activation in brain networks associated with cognitive control and monitoring (increased connectivity between posterior cingulate, dorsal anterior cingulate, and dorsolateral prefrontal cortices) in meditators. The study related the modifications in the DMN to a decrease in mind wandering in meditators. This would suggest that the findings are more relevant to modifications in attentional balance than levels or types of consciousness and this is further supported by the lack of differences across the three mediation types investigated in the study (loving kindness, focused meditation and open monitoring of the contents of the mind). It may also be that the DMN activation is not a sufficiently sensitive brain marker to detect subtle differences in experience across meditation practices and kinds of consciousness employed. Nevertheless, we know that refined attentional skills are a prerequisite for the exploration of more subtle levels of consciousness. It is possible that future research will be able to build on these initial findings and fine-tune questions about the differences in conscious experience of meditators and its coupling with distinct neural correlates to the point where more subtle differences in brain activation will be possible to detect.

The illusory nature of reality

One of the main aspects of mind training at the level of exploration of consciousness in Dzogchen relates to the question of what is real. As the practitioner works more closely with the substrate of individual consciousness and the substrate of reality, a realization emerges that what is often considered to be real is actually unstable, modifiable and arises in dependence on our mind. This view is, at least to some extent, supported by traditional arguments in Western philosophy and current scientific understanding of how our perceptions and representations of the world are created.

For example, when we look at a daisy in front of us the electrical impulses on the retina are in the visual cortex translated into neural patterns corresponding to green color, white color, yellow color and other patterns of neuronal firing assembled into vertical, horizontal and diagonal lines. Our brain at this early stage of perception does not identify the combination of shapes and colors as a daisy. It is only further up in the chain of visual processing that the co-occurring patterns of colors and shapes are constructed into the form of an object, yet still, nothing in the electrophysiological impulses tells us that the particular object is a daisy. This is where concepts – the building blocks of our cognition – step in. They integrate our sensations, perceptions, feelings, thoughts and their combinations into identifiable and manipulable mental units. Simply put, concepts are mental labels representing objects, feelings, perceptions, and ideas. Importantly, as we have seen in the daisy example, concepts are not the same as the entities they represent; they are mental representations detached from actual entities. This has consequences for our understanding of reality.

The ordinary mind tends to identify concepts with the entities they denote without a distinction between the two. An essential initial shift away from the indiscriminate immersion in the ordinary mind and the first step towards understanding of the nature of the mind and reality is the explicit recognition and experiential understanding that mental states are detached from the actual objects, feelings, and sensations they represent. This shift in perspective of mental events is sometimes described as 'de-reification' (Dunne 2012). In Dzogchen distinctions are drawn between different gradients of de-reification, progressing from initial loosening-up of the identification with mental states to the highest levels of non-duality. The gradients may involve a progression from initial understanding that thoughts are not facts, through further development of self-reflective awareness of mental states, progressing on to first intellectual and then experiential realization of the emptiness of self and finally the non-dual state of pristine awareness. The faculties of mindfulness and meta-awareness facilitate initial glimpses of de-reification arising from enhanced attentional stability. These are further expanded through self-reflective practices exploring the fleeting nature of mental phenomena. Accumulation of such experiences leads to loosening-up of the notion of self which is at first still rooted in conceptual distinctions about what self is and isn't. The emptiness of 'self' is further realized through purely experiential comprehension which releases the conceptual constructs of self and non-self. The final stage of pristine awareness experientially surpasses the notions of self through the dissolution of the duality between the observer and the observed and encompasses the realization of the nature of mind and also the nature of reality unmediated by concepts. In this way pristine awareness goes beyond the notion of reification and limitations of concepts.

Dreaming and dying

One set of practices in Dzogchen which helps the practitioner realize the ultimate nature of mind and reality is dream yoga. Training in dream yoga combines daytime and night-time practices. During the day, practitioners are encouraged to examine the reality of their immediate experience and to compare it to the experience they would have in a dream. They also practice meditations cultivating attentional and emotional balance to settle the mind to the point where it is possible to work with the substrate consciousness. Another group of practices invites the practitioner to examine the automatic reactions of the mind consciousness and afflictive consciousness to the extremes of ego-centered emotions such as praise and blame. Finally, in direct preparation for the night-time practice of dream yoga, the adept repeatedly develops the motivation during the day to become lucid while dreaming at night. This intention is amplified through specific practices just before the practitioner falls asleep.

The actual night-time practice of dream yoga proceeds in three main stages (Padmasambhava 1998). In the first stage practitioners train in the ability to become lucid in the dream – knowing that they are dreaming while having a dream. Lucid dreaming develops meta-consciousness in a dream state. Research shows that the ability to become lucid in dreams is indeed trainable and is associated with distinct psychophysiological changes (LaBerge 2002). Once the ability to become lucid in dreams is stabilized, the practitioner uses the lucid dream state to test the nature of dream reality. The adept may try to modify seemingly real aspects of the dream, for example, by changing the size of the appearance of an elephant in the dream. Gradually, these reality tests may include more personal aspects of transformation, such as probing the nature of personal fears and ego-centered tendencies. Such practices work more closely with the subtle tendencies at the level of substrate consciousness. Dream yoga can also become an opportunity to extend the daytime meditation practice into the dream state. Finally, the most advanced practices of dream yoga tap into the nature of the pristine awareness which can arise if the practitioner realizes clear light (Sanskrit: prabhāsvara; Tibetan: wosel) – the innermost essence of consciousness – in deep sleep. In this context, Dzogchen teachings discuss 'the child clear light' which manifests while we are asleep. This is where practices of dream yoga connect with practices at the time of death.

Tibetan Buddhist teachings on dying describe four visions associated with the dissolution of bodily elements and four visions arising with the dissolution of consciousness at the time of death (Varela 1997; Dalai Lama 2002). Physiological changes in the body induce the progression from the vision of a mirage, through the vision of smoke, vision of fireflies and finally vision of a flame of a candle. This is immediately followed by the gradual dissolution of consciousness which proceeds through visions of vivid white mind-sky, vivid red-orange mind-sky, vivid black mind-sky, and ends with the experience of clear light, which is the most subtle level of our mind (Varela 1997; Dalai Lama 2002). When the clear light is recognized as the ground of all consciousness it results in the experience of pristine awareness. Most people with an untrained mind are not aware of the stages of dissolution as they go through the process of dying. Even if they become aware of some of the visions, they do not recognize them for what they are. Interestingly, the same visions arise in our consciousness in a more subtle way when we are falling asleep, and in the reverse order when we are waking up from sleep.

From the perspective of Dzogchen the point of the final dissolution of consciousness at the time of death, when the clear light of our mind manifests, is an opportunity to attain enlightenment if practitioners experimentally recognize the clear light as the ultimate nature of their mind and stabilize this realization giving rise to pristine awareness. The ability to recognize clear light at the time of death typically builds on experiencing glimpses of clear light and pristine awareness in meditation, for example during dream yoga, and this enables the practitioner to recognize the ultimate nature of consciousness when it is fully revealed. When this happens it is said that the mother clear light, the actual full manifestation of clear light at the time of death, meets the child clear light experienced in meditation during life, which culminates in the complete experience of pristine awareness (Dalai Lama 2002). The amount of time practitioners spend in the union of mother and child clear light at the time of death depends on the stability of their concentration and realization – it is claimed to last five times longer than the length of continuous experience of pristine awareness in meditation during life.

Dzogchen texts describe the state of abiding in clear light as a sign of accomplishment in the practice. Advanced masters are often aware of the time of their death and when the time comes they rest their mind in deep meditation until the clear light of their mind fully manifests (Varela 1997). When they experience the union of mother and child clear light, they are able to abide in this state for days, even weeks. During this time their body does not show vital signs, neither does it display signs of decay and often stays in the meditative posture. While such descriptions seem in the Western cultural context unusual, to say the least, many such cases have been documented in the history of Tibetan Buddhism (Khenpo Tsultrim Lodu 2006) and recently noted by some Western doctors witnessing such states (Varela et al. 1991).

Over the last three years I have followed verifiable reports regarding two lamas who stayed in the state of clear light at the time of their death for weeks. While it was not possible for me to conduct direct first-hand research on those cases and therefore the evidence is only anecdotal, I have followed the cases based on witness reports while the lamas were abiding in the state of clear light. Both of these cases occurred in the Kham region of Eastern Tibet. The first one – Chosyang Dorje Rinpoche – was a realized master of Dzogchen and Mahamudra who passed away in April 2010 and his body remained in a meditative position displaying physical signs matching the state of clear light for seven weeks. The second case was Lama Loma, an accomplished master of Dzogchen in the Nyingma lineage of Tibetan Buddhism, who died in October 2011 and, according to witnesses, remained in the clear light state for three weeks. Both of these two yogis predicted their death, entered the process of dying in meditation and manifested additional physiological signs which seem to accompany abiding in the state of clear light at the time of death, such as radical shrinking in body size.

While widely accepted in the tradition of Dzogchen, from the perspective of Western science, where such cases are virtually unknown, these descriptions raise the possibility that meditative states such as abiding in clear light are indeed achievable and are associated with specific physiological markers. Any research which may in the future tap into such states will need to respect the cultural and contemplative context in which these experiences arise. To prevent disruption to the state of clear light, the accomplished practitioner usually instructs his students or family before death not to move or touch their body once they have entered the state of clear light and also provide guidance on how long the state is going to last. Their body typically starts to show signs of decay and does not hold meditative posture when they no longer abide in the clear light state. While highly challenging, if conducted with the needed concern for ethical and cultural sensitivities, research into these remarkable states would have consequences for our understanding of the process of dying, and also for medical, psychological and spiritual approaches to death.

The enlightened mind

While we may accept that Buddhist training in attention and cultivation of wholesome emotions leads to improved well-being, the notion of
enlightenment may be by many considered an unrealistic ideal. Most
current scientific discussions about meditation techniques avoid the
concept of enlightenment – they end with a reference to a ground state of
consciousness from which our experience arises without distinctions
between substrate consciousness and pristine awareness. There is little
elaboration on how to distinguish this state from other similar experiences
or where our meditation practice is to take us in the end. This may be
satisfactory at the beginning of meditation training when many practitioners simply want to improve their mental and physical health, but as
they progress further, questions about the ultimate aim of their practice
become more prominent.

One way to think about enlightenment is in terms of an exceptional
state of well-being arising from a complete balance of virtuous motivation, attention, wholesome emotions and experiential understanding of
the nature of mind. Western psychology has so far exclusively focused
on the excellence of artistic, intellectual and athletic performance.
However, it seems that such genius is in some people associated with
enhanced well-being and in others with profound imbalance of well-being
(Neihart 1999). From the Buddhist point of view, enlightenment is the
ultimate excellence of the human mind manifesting through a radical
transformation of mental functioning. In Dzogchen, there are detailed
accounts of specific changes arising in the enlightened mind. One of the
central aspects of this transformation is a complete dissolution of the
afflictive consciousness. This is the aspect of consciousness associated
with even the most subtle grasping at the notion of an independent self.
Other changes involve transformation of negative emotions of anger,
attachment, jealousy, pride and ignorance into five kinds of enlightened
wisdom.

The account of the five kinds of enlightened wisdom presented here
follows the teachings of Jamgon Mipham (2009) and Longchenpa (2011).
The five kinds of enlightened wisdom or five types of primordial
awareness are usually divided into two groups. The first one includes the
primordial awareness of dharmadhātu, which is the ultimate awareness
beyond the subject–object duality recognizing the nature of mind and
nature of reality. It is no different from rigpa – the pristine awareness.
Dharmadhātu (Sanskrit: dharmadhātu; Tibetan: Chosyang) is the space
or root of existence from which all phenomena arise and the primordial

awareness of dharmadhātu not only realizes the non-existence of an independent 'self', but also recognizes the nature of the observer of the mind and the nature of all phenomena. This ultimate realization ripens when all afflictions linked to delusion and even the most subtle aspects of ignorance are transformed.

The second kind of primordial awareness includes the other four types of primordial awareness and is sometimes called knowledge from the perspective of others. It is the clear understanding of how phenomena appear to the ordinary unenlightened mind and how unenlightened beings can be supported in their striving towards freedom from suffering. The four kinds of primordial awareness are mirror-like awareness, primordial awareness of equality, discriminating primordial awareness and the primordial awareness that accomplishes all actions. The mirror-like awareness perceives all appearances as they arise at the level of ordinary consciousness and substrate consciousness for unenlightened sentient beings, but at the same time recognizes the illusory nature of these appearances. It means that the enlightened being observes all appearances without grasping or rejection. Transformation of the affliction of anger and the substrate consciousness leads to realization of mirror-like awareness. The primordial awareness of equality arises from the transformation of the afflictive consciousness and the affliction of pride. It becomes the source of courage to help all sentient beings equally – without imposing the frameworks of like and dislike on the perceptions of them. The discriminating primordial awareness enables the enlightened being to recognize the needs of sentient beings and the best ways to help them. It manifests when the mind consciousness and the afflictive emotion of craving are transformed into their pure form, which is the discriminating primordial awareness itself. Finally, the primordial awareness that accomplishes all actions arises through simultaneous transformation of the five kinds of sense consciousness and the affliction of jealousy. This awareness underlies the tireless striving of enlightened beings to benefit sentient beings.

Ultimately, the Dzogchen teachings explain that the mind of the Buddha perceives at the same time the unchanging nature of the mind and the illusory appearances as they arise for unenlightened beings. These accounts of the enlightened mind have been provided by meditators who are believed to have experienced such extraordinary states. Their convergence suggests that this most noble transformation of the mind is possible and achievable. From the perspective of Dzogchen its accomplishment is the realization of the highest human potential.

At this point in time, we do not have an answer to the question whether these accomplished states of mental balance can be studied with the methods of Western science. It is clear that the conceptions of the enlightened mind push the boundaries of metaphysics and ontology on which psychology and neuroscience have been built. It would be interesting to explore how the current scientific paradigms in these fields could be expanded to encompass the concept of enlightenment. The first step might be the recognition that the accounts of enlightenment documented in Dzogchen and other contemplative traditions, rather than being infallible mysticism, have been built on converging detailed accounts of actual human experience and concern transformation of the mind through comprehensive mental training.

Practice: Resting in awareness without an object

It is good to start your meditation session with the sequence of practices from the previous chapters. You first position your body in a comfortable posture, making sure that you are relaxed but alert. You may want to settle your body and release any tension you are holding by tightening up and then relaxing your muscles. Five deep in-breaths and out-breaths, with the out-breath being longer, also help to balance the autonomous nervous system in your body. Now you can proceed to contemplations on intention for your practice. After that you may want to spend five minutes on settling your attention through gentle focus on your breath. Consequently, you proceed on to the practices of the four healthy emotions for ten minutes or as long as you feel you need. Now that your body and mind are in a more balanced state at the levels of motivation, attention and emotion, you may begin explorations of consciousness.

Let's start by observing your mind more closely. Instead of focusing on a specific object such as your breath, or engaging in contemplations on a certain topic, this time you simply observe whatever arises in your mind with an alert, gentle, curious and non-judgmental attitude. You may notice that your mind is drawn to some sensations and perceptions in your environment. You simply let the mental activity arise and settle back into the mind consciousness. Similarly for your thoughts – there is no agenda you want to follow; simply observe your thoughts as they emerge and disappear. You approach your feelings and emotions with the same attitude. You may feel that you are the observer simply watching the happenings on the stage of your mind. You can try to let go of elaborations, judgments and emotional engagement with the thoughts. You simply observe whatever arises and let go. If you find yourself following your thoughts, sensations and emotions, the moment you notice this, simply let go and come back to the observer position. As you get more accustomed to the practice and the mental activity settles to some extent, you may try exploring the nature of your mind with simple questions. Where does the mental activity come from? Where does it go? You may notice that you are increasingly more attuned to more subtle mental activity such as feeling tones, dullness and background chatter in your mind. Can you recognize different levels of subtlety of your mental activity? Once your mind becomes even more settled, longer periods without thought may emerge. During those, you stay alert and observe the emerging radiant non-conceptual aspects of consciousness while letting go of any attachment this may create.

You may want to do the core practice for five to ten minutes at the beginning and gradually increase the duration of your sessions as your mind becomes more balanced. As you proceed further, you may start exploring the nature of the observer watching the mind.

Summary: Chapter 5

Consciousness is one of the most interesting, but also one of the least understood, topics of science. From the point of view of biological sciences, the main distinctions about consciousness have been drawn in terms of brain activity linked to vigilance and cognitive arousal in states such as sleep, being awake or in coma. And over the last two decades, neuroscientific research showed that synchronous neural firing and the default mode of brain function are closely linked to conscious experience. But most interesting questions about how conscious experience arises and how it relates to well-being and human potential remain unanswered.

Dzogchen accounts of consciousness are based on refined introspective methods and are closely linked to questions about genuine happiness. Here three main levels of consciousness are distinguished. The ordinary level of consciousness is the mind we experience most of the time until we progress to more advanced stages of contemplative training. Beyond the ordinary mind is a substrate of individual experience that holds imprints of our unconscious tendencies and behavior. As this level of consciousness becomes more calm and balanced, pleasant experiences of bliss, non-conceptuality and clarity may arise. However, inherent in this layer of consciousness is a subtle notion of an independent self. So it is neither the ultimate, nor the purest aspect of our consciousness. Based on Dzogchen teachings, beyond this layer of consciousness abides pristine awareness, which is also described by the attributes of bliss, non-conceptuality and clarity, but these now arise undifferentiated and unmediated by the notion of a separable 'I'. The goal of contemplative training is to recognize and sustain the experience of this level of consciousness.

Practices probing the nature of the mind and reality such as dream yoga help the practitioner realize pristine awareness. In dream yoga, we use lucid dreaming to examine similarities and differences between the dream state and what we perceive as reality. The most advanced practices of dream yoga work with clear light – the innermost essence of consciousness – in deep sleep. Recognition of clear light as the nature of the mind gives rise to pristine awareness. This is where practices of dream yoga connect with practices at the time of death. In the final stages of dying the clear light of mind is revealed and if it is recognized as pristine awareness and this realization is sustained the practitioner reaches enlightenment. In Dzogchen the state of enlightenment is described in terms of five kinds of primordial wisdom which arise through transformation of the afflictions and mental processes associated with afflictive mental activity.

Chapter 6

Implications for the science of meditation and the practitioner

Science and Buddhism: The future of meditation research

Exploration of neural plasticity resulting from meditation-based mind training is arguably one of the most exciting areas of research in current psychology and cognitive neuroscience. Over the last decade we have witnessed a sharp increase in the number of studies into changes in the mind and brain resulting from meditation. Most of this research aimed to document that meditation can indeed lead to tangible modifications in systems of attention and emotion processing, including relevant brain and body physiology. The field is now gradually evolving towards more refined research questions about underlying cognitive and neural mechanisms and differential effects of the type and amount of meditation practice.

Despite this positive development, many fundamental questions about meditation and its impact on the mind and brain remain to be addressed. The role of introspective data in research on meditation is one of them. Refined introspective exploration of the mind is central to most contemplative mind training methods in Buddhism, particularly so in Dzogchen. Because of this focus on conscious experience, questions about the relationship between first-person introspective accounts and changes in mental activity and neural substrates investigated using third-person methods arise more prominently in meditation research than other subareas of psychology and neuroscience. Current research in cognitive neuroscience of meditation mostly ignores indepth inquiries into modifications in introspective conscious experience arising from meditation practice and focuses on the 'easy questions' about neural correlates of meditation. This is evident in most of the studies on changes in attention and emotion processing associated with meditation we have discussed.

In order to develop the field further, meditation research needs to explore ways to capture first-person accounts of conscious experience more closely. Systematic investigation of possible links between traditional theories of Buddhist mind training and established psychological and neuroscientific markers will be instrumental in this development. To start with, it would be useful to examine points of convergence in findings from basic introspective methods relying on questionnaires and different kinds of third-person methods. A recent research study by Jacobs et al. (2011) is a good initial step in the trend towards the acquisition of converging evidence across levels of scientific investigation – from introspection, through measures of cognitive activity and body physiology impacting on cellular changes.

Jacobs et al. (2011) investigated the connections between meditation practice, feelings of purpose in life and mindfulness, emotional processing and hormonal activity linked to well-being. As part of the Shamatha project participants were training in calm-abiding and also practices cultivating positive emotions for approximately six hours a day for three months. A range of cognitive tests assessing changes in attention and emotion processing were performed before, after and also during the three months. Results from the retreat participants were compared with a group of matched controls who underwent the same meditation training at a later time. In addition to tests of attention and emotion processing, the researchers used self-report questionnaires to track modifications in variables such as purpose in life and mindfulness. They also assessed a biological marker, telomerase – a cellular enzyme supporting the development of molecular sequences called telomeres at the end of chromosomes. Previous research showed that decreased levels of telomerase are associated with shorter telomere sequences which are linked to faster aging and proneness to disease (Blackburn 2000). Stress has been shown to decrease the production of telomerase (Epel et al. 2006). The study investigated the possibility that meditation training may be associated with an increase in telomerase levels. It was found that retreat participants' levels of mindfulness and feelings of purpose in life increased after meditation training. The results also showed a decrease in personality traits associated with negative emotions, particularly neuroticism. Most importantly, increased feelings of purpose in life and mindfulness led to an increase in levels of the telomerase enzyme. Through the links between meditation training, affect and beliefs about purpose in life and biological markers, this study brought us closer to understanding the somewhat elusive connections between 'mind variables' acquired using introspection-based questionnaire responses and the 'hard evidence' of biological changes in the body.

There is a strong need for more studies which would link biomarkers to cognitive processing and introspective variables such as well-being, purpose in life, mindfulness, and self-compassion. Not only that, it would be very useful to examine more systematically levels of explanation applied in meditation research and connections between them. This brings us back to the fact that science of meditation is fundamentally a science of conscious experience. As such, it faces the 'hard problem' of consciousness (Chalmers 1995) more visibly than other branches of psychology and cognitive neuroscience. The core question is: How can we relate private 'what it feels like' shifts in well-being arising from meditation practice to reaction times, electrophysiological data or measures of brain physiology which are detached from the experiential aspect of consciousness? One of the main remedies to the 'hard problem' can be the development of bridging principles linking introspective data to other levels of explanation (Chalmers 2004).

Neuroscientific research on meditation-based techniques has so far mainly relied on more or less intuitive associations between questionnaire responses and cognitive, psychophysiological or neural activity. For example, the study by Jacobs et al. (2011) explored correlations between scores on mindfulness, purpose in life and neuroticism questionnaires and telomerase levels. Other studies showed that higher mindfulness scores on a mindfulness questionnaire are associated with less activation in the right amygdala in response to pictures of faces showing emotional expressions (Creswell et al. 2007). And a decrease in depression scores has been linked to increased activations in the somatosensory cortex of the brain in participants trained in mindfulness when they were watching sad video clips (Farb et al. 2010). All these and other similar studies provide new and interesting information about associations between meditation-based training and modifications in the mind and brain. However, these are initial, mostly isolated, explorations of the links between introspective reports and psychophysiological or neural activity. What is needed for the field to move to a more mature level of scientific investigation are general principles of bridging first-person data with measurable changes in the mind and brain which are grounded in theories of contemplative mind training. Let's explore this further in the context of the pyramid of mind training in Dzogchen.

As we have seen in previous chapters, the Dzogchen tradition contains detailed descriptions of changes in mental processing resulting from meditation practice. These theories developed from converging and generalizable introspective observation of meditation practitioners over centuries and can provide a valuable foundation for the investigation of bridging principles between modifications in conscious experience induced by meditation and corresponding third-person assessment of changes in the mind and brain. At the level which cultivates attention skills, the nine stages of attention training present a framework for mapping conscious experience of attentional balance on to specific cognitive and neural systems of attention. Building of bridging principles would connect introspective reports with constructs in Western cognitive theory of the mind. This could, for example, involve pairing of introspective changes in attention at the nine stages with varied involvement and performance patterns in vigilance, sustained attention, selective attention and monitoring. In the next step, additional bridging principles could be used to map the introspective reports via the level of cognitive theory on to neural substrates. Overall, this would result in a more systematic and comprehensive investigation of the impact of meditation training on attention at three main levels of explanation: introspective, cognitive mechanisms and neural substrates. This three-level approach could be further extended by additional mapping of psychophysiological markers such as cortisol (stress-related hormone), telomerase (Jacobs et al. 2011) or immune system responses (Davidson et al. 2003). Grounded in the theory of bridging principles, researchers would be able to postulate hypotheses in terms of the nine stages, taking into account the nature of the training participants receive, its duration and the amount of initial meditation experience. The predictions regarding the stages of attentional balance would in turn help predict likely changes in one or more components of attention, associated brain substrates and links between the different levels of explanation.

A similar approach could be applied to the development of bridging principles at the remaining three levels of the pyramid. With regard to balance in motivation, it would be interesting to investigate how the initial self-focused intentions of a practitioner expand with increased meditation proficiency and how these changes impact on well-being and hormonal markers of physical health. At the level of emotional balance, we could explore bridging principles between the three gradients of compassion and corresponding cognitive and neural changes. In the case of exploration of consciousness, the distinctions between ordinary consciousness, substrate consciousness and pristine awareness could serve as a foundation for mapping between depth of contemplative practice, well-being and changes in synchronicity of brain oscillations or the default mode of brain function. This systemic approach could become a fruitful ground for meditation research rooted in traditional Buddhist accounts based on introspection, yet extending their scope by research using methods of Western science of the mind and brain.

The mind–body problem

There seems to be an upsurge of both expert and lay interest in neural substrates of meditation. Over the last decade brain research on neural plasticity resulting from meditation training made headlines not only in scientific circles, but also in the mainstream press. This trend goes hand in hand with recent advancements in non-invasive brain imaging which enabled us to study the brain online, as it is engaging in brain activity. As a result of these advances, neuroscientific evidence is often regarded as more substantial than evidence provided by other scientific methods. For example, it has been shown that non-experts have the tendency to trust an explanation more if it includes some reference to neuroscientific facts, even if that information is irrelevant (Weisberg et al. 2008). Without a doubt, the new imaging methods substantially expanded the repertoire of scientific tools which are available to researchers in their quest for understanding how the mind and brain work. But it is also important to know about the limitations of these methods, so that we do not overvalue their potential because of their novelty and at the cost of other equally valuable, but perhaps less attractive, sources of knowledge.

The reliance on neuroscientific evidence has particularly strong consequences for research on meditation. This is because of the reductionist nature of research and explanations provided by neuroscience – lay descriptions of neuroscience often say that it is a discipline which studies 'how the brain produces the mind and behavior'. Such emphasis on the brain is in sharp contrast with the focus on conscious experience and reliance on introspective methodology in meditation-based mind training. This discrepancy taps into fundamental questions about the nature of the mind, consciousness and the brain, and their relationship – the mind–body problem. If we believe that our conscious experience which arises from our mind can influence our brain, the question is, how can our mind as an immaterial entity influence and modify something material – our brain? Western science and philosophy have struggled with this problem for centuries and do not have a widely accepted solution. There have been some attempts in Western science to solve the problem through postulation of bridging entities between the mind and the brain (Popper and Eccles 1977). Some recent accounts suggest that the dualistic ontology of quantum physics referring to matter and experiences is the solution to the mind–body problem (Stapp 1996). However, neither of these accounts managed to make its way into mainstream psychological and neuro-scientific research, and the reductionist materialist approach of neuro-science remains predominant.

The mind–body problem points to fundamental differences in ontology between Western science and Buddhism – beliefs about what exists and can be studied by science. While the prevalent view of mind in neuro-science reduces the mind into processes of the brain and postulates that by studying the brain we can understand the mind, from the point of view of Dzogchen, mind cannot be reduced to the brain, even though it can be influenced by the brain. Aspects of consciousness such as the pristine awareness and substrate consciousness do not disappear at the time of death of the brain. They continue to exist after death and are incarnated into another living form in the next life. Such notions are hard to embrace by Western science which focuses on the immediately observable entities measurable by third-person methods.

How can there be a science of meditation which bypasses the funda-mental differences in ontology between Buddhism and Western neuro-science? One possible solution is to ignore phenomena which give rise to questions about ontology and focus on the measurable evidence at hand (Lutz et al. 2007). Following this approach the science of meditation would be able to study changes in attention and emotional balance, as indeed has been the case, but would fall silent on most questions about the nature of the mind, human potential and different types of con-sciousness. This is certainly a viable research position, but it seems that it leaves the essence of the traditional approach to contemplative mind training outside the realm of science.

In search for the solution to the ontological and mind–body problems arising in research on meditation, it might be useful to revisit the intertwined nature of ontology and scientific investigation (Bechtel 1988). The role of ontology is to provide an array of possible phenomena which can be investigated by science and science provides evidence on which phenomena it found to be existing. This in turn affirms or expands the ontology. Western science has not explored the differences between ordinary consciousness, substrate consciousness and pristine aware-ness so far. In contrast, the Dzogchen tradition has been exploring con-sciousness using first-person methods for centuries and based on these observations postulated the existence of three levels of consciousness, and also described experiential visions at the time of death and even states of consciousness after death and before the next incarnation. Since refined introspective method is accepted as a reliable source of knowledge in the

Buddhist psychology of Dzogchen, the descriptions of different levels of consciousness provided sufficient evidence for expansion of Dzogchen ontology to include such mental entities. This shows that some ontological questions may be answered based on scientific methods we trust to deliver the answers about the existence of phenomena. Thus the answer to questions about ontology of consciousness seems to depend on whether Western science can embrace refined introspective methods as reliable scientific tools providing information about the mind and consciousness.

Secular mindfulness-based approaches and the pyramid of mind training in Dzogchen

Mindfulness-based approaches are among very few psycho-educational programs that enhance well-being (Carmody and Baer 2008; Shapiro et al. 2008) and improve quality of life (Nyklíček and Kuijpers 2008). They can positively impact on the well-being of people with mental and psychosomatic conditions and also further enhance the well-being of healthy adults. What psychological mechanisms are responsible for these beneficial changes? The beneficial effects of mindfulness-based interventions on well-being are likely mediated by the acquisition of new skills in relating to challenging experience. Secular mindfulness-based training emphasizes non-judgmental, non-analytical awareness of both pleasant and unpleasant experience. In this way, it increases exposure to unwanted thoughts, sensations and feelings, and decreases rumination – repetitive negative thinking – which is an essential contributor to symptomatology in stress- and anxiety-related disorders. Mindfulness-based training increases the likelihood of early recognition of negative thoughts and habitual reactions and creates space for change to prevent further negative spiraling into maladaptive cognitions and behavior manifesting in conditions such as depression, eating disorders, and addictions (Baer 2003; Frewen et al. 2008). Because of its well-documented beneficial effects, mindfulness training can serve as a powerful and broadly applicable preventive tool increasing resilience and well-being in the population. Indeed, there is a strong interest in implementing mindfulness-based methods in education and the workplace.

It is clear that mindfulness-based interventions positively impact on well-being. They do so through the development of increased awareness of unwholesome ways of thinking and cultivation of the ability to shift the focus away from negative thinking patterns and towards non-elaborative, mostly sensory, conscious experience. These mechanisms resonate with some of the effects of Buddhist mind training we have described which is not surprising given that secular mindfulness-based interventions have their roots in Buddhist meditation techniques. But there are also points of divergence. How do the mindfulness-based approaches map on to the levels of mind training for well-being in the Buddhist context? To explore the similarities and differences more systematically, we can follow the progression of the pyramid of mind training in Dzogchen, starting with the level of motivation.

Some mindfulness teachers emphasize the importance of the ethical foundations of secular mindfulness practices (Kabat-Zinn 2003) and their role in the reduction of suffering. Indeed, intention has been singled out as a separate dimension of secular mindfulness (Shapiro et al. 2006). Training of teachers in mindfulness-based approaches typically entails some element of Buddhist psychology which includes education about mindfulness in the Buddhist context, including Buddhist ethics. There are also good practice guidelines available for teachers of secular mindfulness-based approaches which emphasize ongoing mindfulness practice, further practice development and adherence to a relevant ethical framework which is not specified as Buddhist. However, the training programs for clients do not cover the intention basis of Buddhist mind training. The extent to which the ethical foundations of Buddhist practice are reflected in the delivery of secular mindfulness training often depends on the background of the teacher with many mindfulness teachers training also in one or more of the Buddhist traditions. But the actual secular mindfulness programs as they are delivered to lay participants do not contain explicit discussions about the ethical foundations of mindfulness practice and do not explicitly encourage contemplations on these aspects of meditation. It is outside their scope to teach how the mindfulness training fits into the broader map of mind training for the ultimate liberation from suffering in the Buddhist sense.

The second level of mind training in Dzogchen focuses on stabilization and refinement of attention conceptualized in terms of nine stages. Secular mindfulness-based approaches do not aim to follow this progression since the achievement of high levels of attentional balance is not their goal. The main emphasis is on basic enhancement of attentional stability and the development of non-judgmental meta-awareness in order to improve people's abilities to cope with everyday stress and anxieties. The focus on grounding of attention in non-elaborative sensory experience in mindfulness-based approaches may actually suggest a slight departure from the traditional meaning of mindfulness towards a different mental faculty called 'manasikara' (Analayo 2006). Manasikara is described as 'the initial split seconds of bare cognizing of an object, before one begins to recognize, identify, and conceptualize' (Analayo 2006: 59). Nyanaponika Thera (1962) used the term 'bare attention' for this mental faculty and considered it to be an aspect of mindfulness. In comparison, the concept of bare attention is rarely mentioned in the Tibetan Buddhist tradition and most traditions of Theravāda and Mahāyāna. In addition to bare attention, secular mindfulness-based approaches emphasize the development of meta-cognitive detachment from mental activity, recognition that 'thoughts are not facts' (Teasdale et al. 2002). This is coupled with the cultivation of a non-judgmental attitude which helps loosen the habitual identification with negative thoughts, often excessively critical self-judgments.

With regard to emotional balance, initial evidence shows that increased levels of mindfulness are associated with better ability to regulate emotions (Roemer et al. 2009). In development of emotion regulation skills mindfulness-based approaches build on cultivation of bare attention, meta-awareness of experience and shifting of attention away from elaborative thinking (Bishop et al. 2004). Research shows that mindfulness training decreases perceived negative valence of stimuli (Arch and Craske 2006) and modifies pathological responses of amygdala in anxiety conditions (Goldin and Gross 2010). In the later study, participants with social anxiety disorder were trained in mindfulness-based stress reduction and their brain activity was assessed before and after the training using functional magnetic resonance imaging (fMRI). The particular task they were asked to perform in the MRI scanner involved reading negative self-beliefs such as 'People always judge me'. After reading each self-belief participants were asked to regulate their emotions elicited by the statement either by focusing on breath or by counting backwards from a three-digit number. The results showed a decrease in activation of the amygdala – a brain structure activated in fear and anxiety responses – and an increase in recruitment of attention regions (after mindfulness-based stress reduction (MBSR) training). This is encouraging given that anxiety disorders are typically associated with continuous overactivation of the amygdala.

Now if we compare cultivation of emotional balance in mindfulness-based approaches to training in emotional balance in the Buddhist context, one of the main differences relates to active development of wholesome emotions. As evidenced by research, secular forms of mindfulness lead to development of self-compassion (Neff 2003; Shapiro et al. 2007), but do not target further cultivation of compassion and other wholesome emotions through explicit practices. In contrast, Buddhist approaches emphasize the value of training the mind in wholesome mental states such as loving kindness, compassion, gratitude, and generosity. In Dzogchen, training in wholesome emotions is considered to be essential to cultivation of emotional balance and connects the first three levels of mind training with the final states of exploration of consciousness. Some teachers of mindfulness-based approaches recognize the need for more explicit training in wholesome emotions within secular mindfulness-based approaches, and as a result developed mindfulness-based interventions which incorporate explicit compassion training as their core practice (Neff and Germer 2013).

The final level of mind training, exploration of consciousness, is where secular approaches to mindfulness most significantly depart from Dzogchen. It is outside the scope of mindfulness-based approaches to provide participants with guidance on exploration of deeper roots of their suffering which would lead them to practices investigating the nature of consciousness. Training in secular mindfulness may, however, result in a decentered perspective of the contents of the mind and encourage further self-reflective exploration of the construed notions of the self. These are initial steps in experiential learning of how the ordinary consciousness works and creates our suffering. But both in delivery of the secular programs and in teacher training mindfulness-based approaches do not examine the nature of the observer in relation to the nature of the mind and reality.

The limited scope of secular approaches to mindfulness when it comes to practices and experiences at the level of exploration of consciousness sometimes results in confusion about the goals and realization resulting from mindfulness training. This difficulty is evident in scientific discussions about mindfulness-based approaches where the development of non-elaborative bare attention and decentered perspective of mental activity is sometimes described as direct experience (Teasdale et al. 1995), direct observation (Bishop et al. 2004) and non-conceptual clear awareness (Brown et al. 2007). A lot of caution is needed here. The terms 'direct experience' and 'non-conceptual clear awareness' are used in traditional Dzogchen contexts to describe the ultimate breakdown of the division between subject and object, observer and the observed, at the level of pristine awareness (Dalai Lama 2000). In contrast, the experiences of decentering and bare awareness arise at the level of the ordinary mind, perhaps with some glimpses of the non-conceptual blissful qualities of substrate consciousness when the ordinary mind quiets down to a certain extent. Misinterpretation of experiences across the levels of consciousness may slow down practitioners' progress in meditation-based mind training. For example, we may think that we are experiencing essential aspects of pristine awareness when we are only starting to tap into the substrate consciousness.

Perhaps the differences between levels of mind training, and particularly levels and types of consciousness, outlined in previous chapters may create a framework for placing secular mindfulness-based practices on the continuum of traditional approaches to meditation. The Dzogchen tradition is particularly well positioned for this purpose because of the completeness of accounts about the transformation of the mind on the path and strong emphasis on experiential exploration of the mind rather than religious aspects of practices. Systematic comparisons with traditional approaches to meditation-based mind training may help us understand better the strengths and limitations of secular approaches to mindfulness. Overall, secular mindfulness-based approaches seem to work mostly at the levels of attentional and emotional balance with some initial elements of exploration of consciousness and intention behind the practice. As the field of mindfulness-based training and research develops further, it might be interesting to explore whether secular approaches to mindfulness could be expanded to encompass all four levels of traditional meditation training in more depth. This could inspire expansion of the repertoire of meditation-based techniques applied in secular meditation approaches and also create a basis for further training and development of mindfulness teachers and practitioners.

Dzogchen in Western society

If we compare a person practicing meditation in our modern fast-paced society with the life of a Dzogchen yogi or a yogini in rural Tibet, the differences are many and striking. In general, Buddhism is still looking for the most suitable way of making the depth and complexity of Buddhist mind training accessible to Westerners, despite being broadly introduced into Western culture more than four decades ago. As many previous attempts show, it is difficult to adapt Buddhist teachings and practices to the needs of Western practitioners without either slipping into over-simplification and dogmatism on the one hand or excessive intellec-tualization on the other. So how can Western practitioners train in traditional meditation-based mind training and achieve advanced levels of mental balance as practitioners in the East have done for centuries? Taking the Dzogchen tradition as an example, we can look for answers to this question by exploring the historical introduction of yogic and monastic traditions of Buddhism in Tibet.

Teachings of Buddha Shakyamuni were brought from India to Tibet in the 8th century when Tibetan king Trisong Detsen asked a prominent Buddhist monastic scholar Shantarakshita and the accomplished yogi Padmasabhava to teach Buddhism in his country. Shantarakshita founded the monastic lineage in Tibet. This provided institutional grounding for the translation of Buddhist scriptures into the Tibetan language and for creation of new scholastic works. At the same time, Padmasabhava established the yogic lineage of Tibetan Buddhism teaching non-monastic meditators how to integrate training in advanced meditation practices with family and work responsibilities. The core of Padmasambhava's teachings was Dzogchen.

The final goal of both monastic and yogic practices was to liberate the mind from suffering, but their emphasis was on different practices. The monastic approach was intended for those who wanted to abandon the worldly life and follow the path of renunciation. Their practices were mostly based on sutra teachings which contain specific guidelines on what behaviors and mental states should be abandoned and which qualities of the mind and behavior should be cultivated instead. In the mind training, monastics would mostly rely on the application of antidotes aimed to counter afflictions and on gradual cultivation of positive qualities. For example, in the face of craving, the sutra approach would apply practices which highlight the impurity and impermanence of ordinary pleasures. With the arising of anger, the practitioner would contemplate loving kindness and the interconnectedness of all beings.

In contrast, the yogic lineage focused on teachings of tantra which included yoga of inner energy channels, visualization practices and Dzogchen practices of direct insight into the nature of mind and reality. While leading an active householder life, a yogi would aim to transform any ordinary activity and everything that arises in the mind into an opportunity for meditative mind training. For example, naturally arising feelings of unconditional love towards the yogi's own children or family members would become the foundation for the development of loving kindness and compassion for all beings. During routine ordinary activities, the practitioner would train in attentional balance using mindfulness practices and mantra recitation. And at night, the yogi would use the dream state to explore the nature of mind and reality. The core experiential approaches of the yogi tradition of Dzogchen involved seeing purity in the ordinary rather than rejecting it and realizing that all appearances of the mind arise like a mirage from the pristine awareness.

After their introduction in Tibet, Buddhist teachings transformed many people's lives and according to historical accounts numerous practitioners achieved the highest states of realization (Dudjom Rinpoche 2005). Concrete examples of the positive changes were witnessed at all levels of society, from monastics and lay people to government officials. As a result, Buddhist practice and philosophy became the heart of Tibetan society, which made support and actualization of Buddhist teachings its priority (Powers 1995). This was accomplished through financial and institutional support of monasteries as well as yogis and their centers.

The position of Buddhism in the Western culture is obviously very different. Despite the increasing broad interest in meditation, the role meditation-based mind training plays in our society is marginal in comparison to the traditional Tibetan Buddhist culture. The scholastic role of Tibetan monasteries in the West is mostly served by university-based scholars and secular translation groups. And the vast majority of meditation practitioners in the West are householders. Similarly, most meditation centers can be considered yogic centers because they have been established to serve lay practitioners. Of course, Buddhist monasteries have their place in Western culture and serve those practitioners who decide to forgo a secular lifestyle and want to dedicate themselves to monastic training. But given that most meditation practitioners in the West are householders engaging in meditation practice while pursuing their worldly activities, the yogic approach of Dzogchen may be relevant to this majority. So, despite all the cultural and technological differences, the yogic tradition of Dzogchen, that is more than 1,200 years old, might serve as a model for Western meditation practitioners of the 21st century. These teachings show how to integrate deep meditation practice with the everyday responsibilities of people with families and jobs.

Transforming the mind in everyday life

Given the pressures of our consumerist culture, its continuous focus on pleasure-seeking behavior and the marginalization of genuine happiness and well-being, it may be difficult to sustain meditation practice in everyday life. Somewhat surprisingly, current research on meditation can be helpful in this regard. With the growing scientific and public interest in the effects of meditation training, misconceptions and stereotypes about meditation may gradually change and focused authentic ways of meditation-based mind training, both secular and traditional, may become more broadly accepted and accessible. From the wider long-term perspective, this could encourage a gradual cultural shift in focus from the populist hedonistic views of happiness towards genuine happiness and well-being and also highlight the need for lifestyle changes which are conducive to meditation practice.

What does a lifestyle supportive of contemplative mind training in active life entail? From the perspective of Dzogchen and other Buddhist traditions, one of the main changes in lifestyle requires a reduction in unnecessary distractions – ranging from constant information overload from television, internet and other sources to habitual superficial socialization. Consider how much time we spend every day watching television or the news, chatting on the phone or checking social media sites. If the amount of time spent in these activities could be reduced, this would free up the necessary gaps in our busy schedules which could be dedicated to focused meditation practice. As a result, we might be able to introduce short formal practice sessions of various lengths during the day, from a few minutes to an hour or more.

Another lifestyle modification is not subject to time restrictions – it involves making changes to the ways we approach and do our daily activities. For example, we can turn our morning routine into a practice of intention and attentional focus. In the morning, instead of repeatedly mentally going over all the tasks which are waiting for us, we can start the day mindfully and meaningfully by developing wholesome intentions with a question: How will I train my mind in genuine happiness and well-being today? Then instead of impatiently going through the routine morning activities, we can stay in the moment and ground our attention on the immediate experience of drops of water falling on our body while taking a shower or as we are getting dressed develop an appreciation for the unique opportunity to train in wholesome emotions during the day we are starting. Similarly, we can develop our meta-awareness many times during the day by introspecting the mind, checking the immediate emotional tone, pace of thinking, and habitual focus of our mind. We can cultivate wholesome emotions while we are engaging in a conversation with a colleague at work and, instead of impatience, jealousy, frustration and arrogance, try to respond to everyday challenges with compassion, equanimity and rejoicing. As we progress further in the mind training and start applying more advanced methods of Dzogchen, we may try to face anger, attachment, and ignorance in everyday situations more directly, by experiencing the underlying pure quality of these afflictions as clarity, bliss and non-conceptuality (Padmasambhava 1998). It is very useful to develop an individual plan of how to turn ordinary activity into wholesome mind training, from the moment we wake up until we go to bed, and maybe even at night with practices such as dream yoga. It is also useful to learn how practice in retreat can complement and enhance everyday mind training.

Buddhist meditation is stereotypically associated with a secluded retreat environment, symbolizing renunciation of worldly life. But both the notion of retreat and the concept of renunciation encompass multiple levels of meaning. At a deeper level renunciation represents the resolve to abandon the afflictive mind and the dedication to development of genuine well-being. Such notion of renunciation does not necessarily entail giving up all worldly commitments. Practice in retreat can deepen the sense of renunciation and experiential understanding of the teachings. Therefore, it is useful to incorporate retreat days into contemplative mind training in active worldly life. The retreat could range from five hours in the morning every Sunday to regular weekly retreats several times a year. Whatever the amount of retreat our schedule allows, these more extensive and focused periods of practice can support and revive the everyday mind training. However, for the meditation training to be fully effective, it needs to be applied in every activity, inside and outside the protected retreat environment. This brings us to the more essential meaning of retreat, which really means not being distracted by superficial mental activity. At the advanced levels of mental balance physical seclusion is not necessary for the mind to be continuously 'in retreat' despite the chaos of the outside world.

The considerations about renunciation and retreat link to other aspects of mind training such as diligence and perseverance. The notion of neuroplasticity can be useful here. Meditation-based mind training is closely linked to the ability of the brain to form new neural connections as a result of practice. With repetition, the strength of neural connections underlying our habitual thought patterns, behavior and emotional experience increases (Hebb 1949). The famous statement 'neurons that wire together, fire together' is often used to describe this form of learning. The extent of neural plasticity induced by meditation practice and its lasting impact depend on the initial state of our mind and brain, the type of training we are undertaking and the amount of practice. In other words, meditation-based mind training can be used to decrease symptoms of anxiety as well as to enhance the gradients of wholesome emotions of an already stable mind. We can use meditation-based techniques casually when we experience stress, or practice with diligence to achieve advanced levels of mental balance. Several neuroscientific studies have shown that the effects of meditation on the balance of the mind and brain depend on the amount of practice (Brefczynski-Lewis et al. 2007). Learning any skill takes time and practice; transformation of the mind and rewiring of the brain for genuine well-being through contemplative mind training are no exceptions – they require effort, diligence and perseverance.

However, traditional Buddhist sources also emphasize the importance of quality, not only quantity, of meditation (Patrul Rinpoche 1998). This relates to challenges in assessment of the progress in meditation practice and is an important area of future research into the effects of meditation. Hours of practice are clearly important, but if the practitioner slips into a dull routine in meditation sessions, it is possible to spend years practicing, without the transformational effects of meditation taking place. So the practitioner should not only focus on the amount of time spent in practice but also check the quality of the practice and its progress. Guidance from a qualified teacher is instrumental in this process. The issue of quantity versus quality is relevant to meditation practitioners in both Buddhist and secular contexts.

Another challenge the practitioner may encounter is associated with unusual, often pleasant, blissful experiences that might arise as one progresses in meditation training. In Dzogchen, this becomes particularly relevant when we proceed to more advanced stages of attentional stability and start exploring the three layers of consciousness. Such experiences are usually side-effects of balancing adjustments the mind and body go through in the process of contemplative mind training. They typically do not have a special significance, but can become a source of distraction – a sidetrack creating craving for more blissful experience. Some practitioners may also confuse these experiences for profound insights and even final achievements. The safeguards against such obstacles are familiarity with the progression of mind training and corresponding differences in conscious experience coupled with guidance from a qualified teacher. But finding an authentic path and a qualified teacher can be a challenge in itself. Here it can be useful to examine first whether the school or tradition we choose to follow is authentic and helped others achieve advanced levels of mental balance. Similarly, a qualified teacher would not only have scholastic understanding of meditation teachings and practices, but would also demonstrate a solid experiential realization of the teachings as reflected in the transformation of the teacher's own mind.

Development of mental balance and well-being in active life using meditation-based mind training is certainly challenging. Some of the requirements we have highlighted relate to changes to our lifestyle, commitment to the practice, diligence and perseverance and proper guidance. It is perhaps useful to emphasize that every moment we spend in meditation counts and helps us transform the mind for the better. It can also be helpful to study how practitioners in the past, for example yogis of the Tibetan tradition of Dzogchen, achieved very advanced levels of well-being and balance in active householder life. This can serve as an encouragement and inspiration for us to revive and explore such an approach in modern Western society. Obviously, the situation of contemporary practitioners in the West is not the same as the conditions of Dzogchen practitioners centuries ago – while we are faced every day with countless distractions which can scatter the equilibrium of our mind, we can also rely on new sources of information which can enhance our practice. As the research in psychology and neuroscience of meditation develops further, it provides new insights into the evolution of a practitioner's mind through contemplative mind training. This can be particularly illuminating for Western practitioners struggling with cultural translations of traditional Buddhist systems of mind training and their adaptation to Western lifestyle.

Conclusion: Enlightenment as an exceptional level of mental balance

At one point or another in their lives, most people start asking questions about how to achieve more balance, contentment and peace, how to be more happy. As we move through life's challenges our answers to these questions change. We may be trying to find happiness in our work, relationships, hobbies, possessions. But when we look back, we often observe a repeated pattern. We find that once we achieve one thing that is supposed to make us happy, we think of something else that could make us even happier! While all these ways of searching for happiness have their place in our life, they obviously do not provide the final answer to the question about happiness we have started with.

So how can we achieve genuine happiness and lasting balance? According to Buddhist teachings the key to lasting happiness is mental balance achieved through mind training. This ancient approach is getting increasingly more support from current scientific studies on the effects of meditation on our mind and brain. Psychological research shows that meditation-based mind training enhances well-being (Carmody and Baer 2008), reduces stress, anxiety, and neuroticism, and improves mood (Jacobs et al. 2011). In addition, neuroscientific and psychophysiological studies show that these changes are associated with enhanced efficiency of attentional processing (Slagter et al. 2007), a decrease in responsiveness of brain structures sensitive to anxiety and fear (Goldin and Gross 2010), and better immune system functioning (Davidson et al. 2003). These initial findings lend support to traditional Buddhist accounts of happiness and mental balance which we have explored from the perspective of the Dzogchen tradition.

Based on the teachings of Dzogchen there are four intertwined facets of mental balance: balance of intention and motivation, attentional balance, emotional balance and balance arising from exploration of consciousness. Balance of attention means being able to choose what we want to focus on, sustaining attention on the object of our attention and noticing when we get distracted. In this way our mind is much less often automatically drawn towards sensations, perceptions, emotions and thoughts which immediately catch its attention without meta-awareness. Through training in mindfulness and meta-awareness it is possible to make the attention skills more stable and serviceable. This gives us the choice to decide what we want to focus on and for how long, rather than our mind choosing or shifting the focus of our attention based on habitual tendencies and attractiveness or rejection of stimuli entering our senses. We may no longer get caught up in useless repetitive thinking about an event or a person – in rumination which can lead to a spiral of negative thoughts. Training of attention enables the practitioner to break through such unhelpful patterns and enables the attention to be placed evenly where it is needed and in a way that brings grounding and calm to the immediate experience.

Emotional balance is closely related to balance of attention. If the practitioner is not able to stabilize attention in situations that are emotionally neutral, working with angry or anxious experiences can become overwhelming. Trained and refined attention skills make it possible for us to recognize circumstances in which we are likely to lose emotional balance and habitual thought patterns which contribute to this. They enable us to pause before the cycle of unwholesome reactivity manifests itself in its full force. Pliant attention makes it also possible to engage in practices which cultivate healthy emotions such as generosity, loving kindness, compassion, rejoicing and equanimity. These in turn counter the negative tendencies of the mind and develop wholesome ways of responding to challenging experience.

In Dzogchen, the training in attentional and emotional balance needs to be built on a solid foundation of wholesome motivation and values. The notions of values and ethics are often not well received – particularly in connection to meditation, the concept of ethics may sound dogmatic. Ethics, intention and related terms are often associated with unhelpful boundaries and restrictions. However, the motivational foundation of meditation practice in Dzogchen does not impose artificial rules and prescriptions. Rather, the intention aspect of mind training invites exploration of the basic human need for purpose, meaning, and genuine happiness, in connection with universal rules of no harm to oneself and others, and aspirations to care and be of help. These contemplations support the practices of attentional and emotional balance. Buddhist writings mention examples of how motivation impacts on meditation practice and how it can enhance or impede the practitioner's progress (Padmasambhava 1998; Patrul Rinpoche 1998). In the practice of Dzogchen and other Buddhist schools, wholesome motivation behind the wish to achieve mental balance is central to meditation training and translates into balance of practitioner's activity and behavior. This means being able to distinguish with clarity harm from non-harm, virtue from non-virtue, and based on that, act and behave in wholesome ways, further sustaining and developing the attentional, emotional and motivational balance.

Finally, it may be useful to summarize the link between enlightenment and balance at the levels of motivation, attention and emotion. In the context of Dzogchen enlightenment could be viewed as an exceptional state of mental balance, as a culmination of mind training at the four levels. From this perspective we could say that Buddha Shakyamuni and others who achieved enlightenment were practitioners who brought the balance of their minds to perfection. They achieved complete pliancy of attention; their emotional balance was such that even the most subtle forms of afflictive mental states would not arise in their minds because they had abandoned the afflictive mind which is the source of ego-centered clinging. And most importantly, their balance of motivation, attention and emotions enabled them to explore levels of consciousness beyond the ordinary mind. Through their experiential understanding of how the mind works they were able to connect with, recognize and stabilize their mind at the most subtle level of our consciousness – the pristine awareness. Abiding in this non-conceptual subtly blissful state of clarity which dissolves the dualistic divisions between the subject and the object, they were able to perceive at the same time the true nature of reality and the dualistic illusory appearances arising for unenlightened beings at the level of ordinary consciousness (Padmasambhava 1998). Tibetan Buddhist teachings describe that, guided by the ultimate understanding of virtue and non-virtue and needs of others, enlightened beings apply their minds and activity to what is of best benefit to beings from the space of unconditional loving kindness and compassion (Dzogchen Ponlop Rinpoche 2004).

Such descriptions of enlightenment may sound intriguing, yet enlightenment in Western culture is mostly perceived as an unachievable idealistic goal. As we approach such claims with healthy skepticism it can be helpful to highlight that Buddhist attitude to development of mental balance is strictly empirical. Rather than accepting or rejecting claims about enlightenment in principle, we may try to put them to the practical test. As the example of mind training in the Dzogchen tradition explored in previous chapters shows, teachings based on experiential accounts of practitioners who achieved the highest levels of mental balance outline the steps and practices of the path. It is up to us to find out both in our own experience and through scientific research whether they can lead to the most subtle levels of mental balance.

There are no quick fixes on the path of contemplative mind training. Just like learning any other skill, training in mental balance requires proper guidance, dedication, time and effort. This is hardly surprising considering how long it takes and how arduous it is to learn to read and write, not to speak about studying for a university degree. It would be interesting to investigate the impact on our well-being and happiness if a similar amount of practice was dedicated to training in attentional, emotional, motivational balance and exploration of the nature of our mind. Maybe it is time to move the notions of enlightenment and the path to it from the realm of mysticism to the realm of empirical examination both at the personal level and from the perspective of science. In such investigation the object of the study would be our own mind and the possibilities of its trainability for balance, genuine happiness and well-being. According to the teachings of Dzogchen, we might realize that the source of ultimate happiness is to be found within our mind and the path to it is within our reach.

Summary: Chapter 6

Research on effects of meditation on the mind and brain has so far provided clear evidence that meditation-based mind training can lead to measurable changes in cognitive performance and brain substrates. Now the field is moving towards more specific questions about the mechanisms underlying such changes. In this research converging evidence acquired at different levels of explanation, such as coupling of introspective reports with measurable changes in brain and body physiology, is particularly valuable. In order to make further progress in research on meditation, we need to develop bridging principles between the different levels of explanation which would guide researchers in the postulation of more fine-grained hypotheses about how meditation impacts on the mind and brain. The outline of the four levels of mind training in Dzogchen may provide an initial inspiration for the development of such principles. For example, the distinctions of nine stages of attentional balance and three gradients of compassion may be the starting point for an exploration of corresponding modifications in subsystems of attention and emotion processing and their links.

The central involvement of introspective methodology in meditation-based mind training also raises fundamental questions about the relationship between mind and brain. While neuroscientific evidence is highly valued in the field of meditation research and beyond, its approach is fundamentally reductionist – aiming to explain fully the changes in conscious experience of meditation practitioners in terms of neural activity. This is in striking contrast to the traditional Buddhist psychology built solely on introspective evidence. This contradiction in methodologies highlights the underlying problem of what phenomena exist and can be studied by science (ontology) and how an immaterial entity such as the mind can impact on the material brain. It might be that the ontological question is actually a question about what scientific methodology we consider to be reliable enough to restrict the ontological options about the mind and brain. If we think that Buddhist introspective accounts are scientifically valid, we may also be able to accept their ontology, which includes postulation of levels of consciousness and subtle distinctions between attentional and emotional balance.

Given the popularity and broad applicability of mindfulness-based interventions which have their origins in Buddhist meditation techniques, it can also be interesting to explore how training in these secular approaches to mindfulness maps on to the four levels of mind training in Dzogchen. It seems that most secular mindfulness programs train the mind at foundational levels of attentional and emotional balance. Their employment of the levels of motivation and exploration of consciousness is fairly limited. Perhaps the scope of the secular approaches to mindfulness, both at the level of intervention delivery and teacher training, could be meaningfully expanded by additional meditation techniques working with each of the four levels.

Finally, we can explore the progression of mind training in Dzogchen from the perspective of a Western meditation practitioner. How can this form of meditation-based mind training be implemented in the busy lives of Western practitioners with family and job commitments? To answer this question, we have revisited the early days of Buddhism in Tibet 12 centuries ago and particularly focused on the beginnings of the yogic lineage which followed the path of Dzogchen. This traditional example of skillful integration of mind training in Dzogchen with everyday activities can be a source of inspiration for contemporary householder practitioners in the West. It requires development of a lifestyle which is conducive to meditation practice, including reduction in distractions from information overload, systematic implementation of meditation practices in everyday activities combined with formal practice and retreat. Maybe it is time to put to the empirical test the outlined possibilities of cultivating mental balance at the four levels in everyday life. This includes demystification of the notion of enlightenment which can be from the Dzogchen perspective conceptualized as an exceptional level of mental balance and the ultimate fulfillment of human potential.

Glossary

Abhidharma (Pāli: Abhidhamma; Sanskrit: Abhidharma)   Buddhist texts containing philosophical considerations about the mind and taxonomies of mental phenomena.

Affect   in the context of cognitive psychology and cognitive science, an overarching category which includes emotions, moods, impulses and stress.

Amygdala   almond-shaped brain structures located in the medial temporal lobes and involved in affective reactions such as fear.

Anterior cingulate cortex (ACC)   area of the brain involved in regulation of emotions and decision making.

Arousal   in the context of emotion research, reflects the intensity of emotional experience.

Attention blink   describes the limited attentional capacity of the mind to detect stimuli occurring too close together in time (within 500 ms), which often results in the second stimulus of a sequence not being noticed.

Behaviorism   school of psychology focusing on investigation of observable behavior rather than processes of the mind.

Bhūmi (Sanskrit: Bhūmi; Tibetan: byang chub sems dpai sa)   levels of accomplishment in contemplative training on the path to complete enlightenment; the Mahāyāna tradition usually describes 11 Bhūmis; teachings of Dzogchen often discuss 16 Bhūmis.

Boddhicitta   a quality of the mind which directly links contemplative mind training to the goal of enlightenment. It is often divided into relative and absolute bodhicitta. Relative bodhicitta is the mental state of strong aspiration to attain enlightenment and help all sentient beings achieve this state, which translates into dedicated engagement in mind training leading to it. Absolute bodhicitta is the state of recognizing the nature of the mind and stabilizing consciousness in this mental state, which is the same as enlightenment.

Boddhisattva   a being who vows to work tirelessly to free all beings from suffering after reaching own liberation.

Clear light (Sanskrit: prabhāsvara; Tibetan: wosel)   the innermost essence of consciousness, manifesting in deep sleep and in final stages of the dissolution process at the time of death; recognition of clear light leads to the experience of pristine awareness.

Cognition   a broad category encompassing mental processes involved in perception, thought, language, decision making and affective processing.

Cognitive neuroscience   a branch of neuroscience examining the links between mental processing and brain structure and functioning in humans.

Cognitive science   an interdisciplinary science of the mind integrating research in cognitive psychology, cognitive neuroscience, philosophy of mind and science, linguistics, computer science and cognitive anthropology.

Contemplative   referring to contemplative practice which involves a range of mind training methods, mostly meditation, used in spiritual philosophies and religious traditions.

Contemplative science   an interdisciplinary branch of science integrating research in philosophy, religious studies, psychology and neuroscience in investigation of the impact of contemplative practice on the mind and brain.

Corrugator supercilii   facial muscle located between the eyebrows and involved in frowning; increased activity in this muscle is associated with unpleasant affect.

Default mode network (DMN)   a network of brain areas which are active when people are resting with eyes closed or focusing on a fixation point. DMN activation is a marker of interconnectedness in activation across brain regions in a resting state.

Defense mechanisms   mental strategies such as rationalization protecting the self from feelings of guilt or shame.

Dharmadhātu (Sanskrit: dharmadhātu; Tibetan: Chosyang)   in Dzogchen is the space or root of existence from which all phenomena arise.

Dorsolateral prefrontal cortex   area of the brain involved in functions of executive control, particularly working memory, aspects of attention monitoring and decision making.

Dzogchen a tradition of Tibetan Buddhism which focuses on direct understanding of the innate pristine nature of awareness; within the system of Tibetan Buddhism Dzogchen is classified as the highest of the teachings (Ati-yoga). It is often described as a group of practices focusing on non-duality.

Electroencephalography (EEG) neuroscientific research method which records electrical activity of the brain (on the scale of microvolts) in the form of oscillations reflecting firing of neural assemblies.

Emotion regulation the ability to modulate processing and expression of emotions.

Emotions one of the subcategories of affect experienced for a shorter amount of time than moods, often in response to a specific event.

Eudaimonic happiness is found in the pursuit of something worthy in the deeper sense; this type of happiness comes from accomplishing our highest potential, from looking for meaning in life and experiences beyond the self-centered perspective.

Event-related potentials (ERPs) averaged brain wave patterns elicited by a certain type of stimulus (e.g. affective pictures or words); ERPs have excellent temporal resolution – they are able to record the brain's activity with millisecond accuracy, but do not provide very specific information about the brain structures producing the electrical signal.

Existentialism philosophical tradition and psychotherapeutic approach explaining how attribution of meaning determines the direction of human life.

Facial electromyography (EMG) records modifications in tension of facial muscles which can be used as physiological markers of the valence aspect of affective experience.

First-person methods (introspective methods) methods investigating functioning of the mind in which research participants observe mental processes in their own mind and report on this.

Five types of primordial wisdom describe the enlightened mind. They include primordial awareness of dharmadhātu, mirror-like awareness, primordial awareness of equality, discriminating primordial awareness and the primordial awareness that accomplishes all actions.

Frontal lobes large areas of the brain located in the frontal parts of the two brain hemispheres; their functioning mediates complex mental processes, including planning, decision making, working memory, attention control and monitoring, and coordination of complex movement.

Functional magnetic resonance imaging (fMRI)   brain imaging method based on metabolic changes in the blood (blood oxygenation level-dependent (BOLD) signal) in response to cognitive demands. This method has very good spatial resolution (in terms of millimeters), but relatively poor timing specificity.

Gray matter of the brain   mainly contains brain cell bodies and receptive branches of neurons.

Hard problem   describes the difficulty in investigating subjective conscious experience, the phenomenological element of consciousness, because of its unique accessibility by the person having the experience which greatly limits comparisons across people and possibilities of scientific investigation into the conscious experience itself.

Hedonistic happiness   derived from pleasure, typically short-lived and bound to particular pleasurable stimuli or circumstances.

Insula   area in the cortex of the brain involved in awareness of emotions and sensations in the body.

Introspection   method of exploring the mind based on observation of our own mental processes.

Mahāyāna   set of Buddhist teachings emphasizing the Boddhisattva ideal which are predominant in Tibet, China, Vietnam and Japan.

Meta-awareness (Pāli: sampajañña; Sanskrit: samprajanya; Tibetan: shizhin)   the monitoring element of attention, which checks the quality of focus on the object of meditation and notices distraction.

Mindfulness (Pāli: sati; Sanskrit: smṛti; Tibetan: trenba)   in the Buddhist context it is a faculty of the mind which enables the practitioner to sustain attention on the object of meditation; in Buddhism mindfulness is associated with prospective memory – remembering to pay attention to the object of meditation. In secular approaches mindfulness is described more broadly as non-judgmental awareness focused on the present moment.

Mindfulness-based approaches   a group of secular programs and therapeutic approaches in which mindfulness is the central component; these most notably include mindfulness-based stress reduction and mindfulness-based cognitive therapy. There are other approaches, such as dialectic behavior therapy and acceptance commitment therapy, in which mindfulness is a therapeutic element.

Mindfulness-based cognitive therapy (MBCT)   is an eight-week secular program combining mindfulness training with elements of cognitive behavioral therapy; MBCT was specifically developed for the treatment of recurrent depression.

Mindfulness-based stress reduction (MBSR) an eight-week secular program developed by Jon Kabat-Zinn which involves a variety of mindfulness practices, education about stress, group discussions about conscious experience, and yoga-based practices. The MBSR laid the foundation for other mindfulness-based approaches.

Mood in comparison to emotions, a more general emotional state lasting for days or weeks.

Neural plasticity describes the modifiability of neural connections, and more broadly, brain function and structure, by experience.

Neurotransmitters chemicals produced by the brain which support communication between neurons.

Ontology in the context of science, ontology restricts the set of entities which can be studied by scientific tools and explanations which are considered plausible.

Orbitofrontal cortex (OFC) area in the prefrontal cortex of the brain involved in decision making and particularly in reward-related processing; imbalance may contribute to development of addictions.

Ordinary mind in the context of Dzogchen, one of the three levels of consciousness which includes sensations, perceptions, thoughts, memories and affect that we typically experience and can mostly become aware of if we observe the mind. These mental processes enable us to learn new skills, make decisions, and function efficiently in everyday life.

Precuneous a brain structure implicated in conscious experience.

Prefrontal cortex the most frontal part of the frontal lobes of the brain excluding motor cortex of the frontal lobes.

Pristine awareness (Sanskrit: vidyā; Tibetan: rigpa) in Dzogchen it is the most subtle aspect of consciousness; the final goal of Dzogchen practices is to access and experientially recognize this type of consciousness and sustain awareness at this ever-present level of ultimate mental balance.

Reductionism is an ontological position which in the context of cognitive neuroscience suggests that the mind can be explained in terms of brain function and structure.

Second-person methods method of investigating the mind in which an experienced meditation teacher uses extensive personal introspective experience in meditation in the assessment and support of adepts on the path.

Self-actualization   satisfaction arising from accomplishing one's potential in terms of talent, abilities and skills; involves mastery of and engaging in activities we enjoy without expectations of recognition from others.

Shamatha (Pāli: samatha, Sanskrit: śamatha or shamatha; Tibetan: shyiné)   aspect of Buddhist mind training concerned with the cultivation of stability, monitoring and redirecting qualities of attention; sometimes referred to as calm abiding.

Skin conductance (electrodermal activity)   reflects modifications in electrical conductivity of the skin caused by increases or decreases in skin moisture resulting from sweating.

Substrate consciousness (Sanskrit: ālayavijñāna; Tibetan: kun gzhi nams shes)   is the second out of the three layers of consciousness described in the Dzogchen tradition. This layer of consciousness contains more subtle tendencies of behavior, mental habits and temper which influence the ordinary mind. It contains the roots of mental frameworks which underlie our construed notions of 'self' or 'I'.

Theravāda   considered the oldest school of Buddhism and predominant in Southeast Asia.

Third-person methods   research tools such as those used in cognitive neuroscience which produce quantifiable and replicable data if researchers apply the same research methods and procedures.

Vajrayāna (Tantrayāna)   a branch of Buddhism prevalent in Tibet which focuses on practices involving sacred visualizations, mantra recitation and work with energies of the body.

Valence   places an emotion on a scale from positive to negative (pleasant to unpleasant).

Visual cortex   areas of the brain involved in visual processing.

Vipassana (Pāli: vipassana; Sanskrit: vipasyana; Tibetan: lhaktong)   practices in which the meditator watches as thoughts, perceptions and emotions arise and fade away, and gradually explores the source of mental activity and its characteristics.

Zygomatic major muscle   facial muscle which controls smiling and shows increased activity during pleasant affect.

Bibliography

Analayo (2006) *Satipatthana: The Direct Path to Realization*, Birmingham: Windhorse Publications.

Arch, J.J. and Craske, M.G. (2006) 'Mechanisms of mindfulness: Emotion regulation following a focused breathing induction', *Behaviour Research and Therapy* 44, 12: 1849–1858.

Aristotle (1985) *Nichomachean Ethics*, Indianapolis, IN: Hackett.

Baer, R.A. (2003) 'Mindfulness practice as a clinical intervention: A conceptual and empirical review', *Clinical Psychology: Science and Practice* 10: 125–143.

Bechtel, W. (1988) *Philosophy of Science: An Overview for Cognitive Science*, Hillsdale: Lawrence Erlbaum Associates.

Bishop, S.R., Lau, M., Shapiro, S., Carlson, L., Anderson, N.D., Carmody, J., Segal, Z.V., Abbey, S., Speca, M., Veltin, D. and Devins G (2004) 'Mindfulness: A proposed operational definition', *Clinical Psychology: Science and Practice* 11: 230–241.

Blackburn, E.H. (2000) 'Telomere states and cell fates', *Nature* 408: 53–56.

Bradley, M.M. and Lang, P.J. (2000) 'Measuring emotion: Behavior, feeling, and physiology', in R.D. Lane, L. Nadel, G.L. Ahern, J.J.B. Allen, A.W. Kaszniak, S.Z. Rapcsak and G.E. Schwartz (eds.) *Cognitive Neuroscience of Emotion* (pp. 242–276), New York, NY: Oxford University Press.

Brefczynski-Lewis, J.A., Lutz, A., Shaefer, H.S., Levinson, D.B. and Davidson, R.J. (2007) 'Neural correlates of attentional expertise in long-term meditation practitioners', *Proceedings of the National Academy of Sciences* 104: 11483–11488.

Brewer, J.A., Worhunsky, P.D., Gray, J.R., Tang, Y.Y., Weber, J. and Kober, H. (2011) 'Meditation experience is associated with differences in default mode network activity and connectivity', *Proceedings of the National Academy of Sciences* 108, 50: 20254–20259.

Brown, K.W., Ryan, R.M. and Creswell, J.D. (2007) 'Mindfulness: Theoretical foundations and evidence for its salutary effects', *Psychological Inquiry* 18: 211–237.

Cahn, B.R. and Polich, J. (2009) 'Meditation (Vipassana) and the P3a event-related brain potential', *International Journal of Psychophysiology* 72: 51–60.

Car, L., Iacoboni, M., Dubeau, M.-C., Mazziotta, J.C. and Lenzi, G.L. (2003) 'Neural mechanisms of empathy in humans: A relay from neural systems for imitation to limbic areas', *Proceedings of the National Academy of Science* 100, 9: 5497–5502.

Carmody, J., and Baer, R. A. (2008) 'Relationships between mindfulness practice and levels of mindfulness, medical and psychological symptoms and well-being in a mindfulness-based stress reduction program', *Journal of Behavioral Medicine* 31,1: 23–33.

Carvera, C.S., Scheier, M.F. and Segerstrom, S.C. (2010) 'Optimism', *Clinical Psychology Review* 30: 879–889.

Cavanna, A.E. and Trimble, M.R. (2006) 'The precuneus: A review of its functional anatomy and behavioural correlates', *Brain* 129: 564–583.

Chalmers, D. (1995) 'Facing up to the problem of consciousness', *Journal of Consciousness Studies* 2: 200–219.

Chalmers, D. (2004) 'How can we construct a science of consciousness?', in M. Gazzaniga (ed.) *The Cognitive Neurosciences III*, Cambridge, MA: MIT Press.

Chomsky, N. (1959a) 'On certain formal properties of grammars', *Information and Control* 2, 2: 137–167.

Chomsky, N. (1959b) 'A review of BF Skinner's Verbal Behavior', *Language* 35,1: 26–58.

Cloninger C.R., Przybeck T.R., Svrakic D.M. and Wetzel R.D. (1994) *The Temperament and Character Inventory (TCI): A Guide to its Development and Use*, St. Louis: Washington University Center for Psychobiology of Personality.

Corbetta, M. and Shulman, G.L. (2002) 'Control of goal-directed and stimulus-driven attention in the brain', *Nature Reviews Neuroscience* 3: 201–215.

Cota, D., Tschöpa, M.H., Horvath, T.L. and Levine, A.S. (2006) 'Cannabinoids, opioids and eating behavior: The molecular face of hedonism?', *Brain Research Reviews* 51: 85–107.

Creswell, J.D., Way, B.M., Eisenberger, N.I. and Lieberman, M.D. (2007) 'Neural correlates of dispositional mindfulness during affect labelling', *Psychosomatic Medicine* 69: 560–565.

Dalai Lama, H.H. (2000) *Dzogchen*, Ithaca, NY: Snow Lion Publications.

Dalai Lama, H.H. (2002) *Advice on Dying*, New York, NY: Atria Books.

Davidson R.J., Kabat-Zinn J., Schumacher J., Rosenkranz M., Muller D., Santorelli S.F., et al. (2003) 'Alterations in brain and immune function produced by mindfulness meditation', *Psychosomatic Medicine* 65: 564–570.

Dorjee D. (2010) 'Kinds and dimensions of mindfulness: why it is important to distinguish them', *Mindfulness* 1, 3: 152–160.

Draganski, B., Gaser, C., Busch, V., Schuierer, G., Bogdahn, U. and May, A. (2004) 'Neuroplasticity: Changes in grey matter induced by training', *Nature* 427: 311-312.

Dudjom Rinpoche (2005) *The Nyingma School of Tibetan Buddhism: Its Fundamentals and History*, Boston, MA: Wisdom Publications.

Dunne, J. (2012) *Mindfulness and Cognition from the Perspective of Buddhist Scholarship,* paper presented at International Symposia for Contemplative Studies, Denver, CO.

Dzogchen Ponlop Rinpoche (2004) *Trainings in Compassion*, Ithaca, NY: Snow Lion Publications.

Ekman, P., Davidson, R.J., Ricard, M. and Wallace, B.A. (2005) 'Buddhist and psychological perspectives on emotions and well-being', *Current Directions in Psychological Science* 14, 2: 59–63.

Engel, A.K. and Singer, W. (2001) 'Temporal binding and the neural correlates of sensory awareness', *Trends in Cognitive Sciences* 5: 16–25.

Epel, E.S., Lin, J., Wilhelm, F.H., Wolkowitz, O.M., Cawthon, R., Adler, N.E., Dolbier, C., Mendes,W.B. and Blackburn, E.H. (2006) 'Cell aging in relation to stress arousal and cardiovascular disease risk factors', *Psychoneuroendocrinology* 31: 277–287.

Farb, N.A.S., Anderson, A.K., Mayberg, H., Bean, J., McKeon, D. and Segal, Z.V. (2010) 'Minding one's emotions: Mindfulness training alters the neural expression of sadness', *Emotion* 10: 25-34.

Forster, K.I. (2004) 'Category size revisited: frequency and masked priming effects in semantic categorization', *Brain and Language* 90: 276–286.

Frankl, V.E. (1966) 'Self-transcendence as a human phenomenon', *Journal of Humanistic Psychology* 6: 97–106.

Frankl, V.E. (2006) *Man's Search for Meaning*, Boston, MA: Beacon Press (first published in 1946).

Fredrickson, B.L. and Joiner, T. (2002) 'Positive emotions trigger upward spirals toward emotional well-being', *Psychological Science* 13, 2: 172–175.

Frewen, P.A., Evans, E.M., Maraj, N., Dozois, D.J.A. and Partridge, K. (2008) 'Letting go: mindfulness and negative automatic thinking', *Cognitive Therapy Research* 32: 758–774.

Frijda, N.H. (2001a) 'Antecedents and functions of emotional episodes', in A.W. Kaszniak (ed.) *Emotions, Qualia, and Consciousness* (pp. 344–362), New Jersey: World Scientific.

Frijda, N.H. (2001b) 'The nature and experience of emotions', in A.W. Kaszniak (ed.) *Emotions, Qualia, and Consciousness* (pp. 344–362), New Jersey: World Scientific.

Gethin, R. (1998) *Foundations of Buddhism*, Oxford: Oxford University Press.

Goetz, J.L., Keltner, D. and Simon-Thomas, E. (2010) 'Compassion: An evolutionary analysis and empirical review', *Psychological Bulletin* 136, 3: 351–374.

Goldin, P.R. and Gross, J.J. (2010) 'Effects of mindfulness-based stress reduction (MBSR) on emotion regulation in social anxiety disorder', *Emotion* 10: 83-91.

Goleman, D. (ed.) (2003) *Destructive Emotions: A Scientific Dialogue with the Dalai Lama*, New York, NY: Bantam Books.

Goodman, A. (2008) 'Neurobiology of addiction: An integrative review', *Biochemical Pharmacology* 75: 266-322.

Hamilton, J.P. and Gotlib, I.H. (2008) 'Neural substrates of increased memory sensitivity for negative stimuli in major depression', *Biological Psychiatry* 63, 12: 1155–1162.

Hebb, D.O. (1949) *Organization of Behavior*, New York, NY: Wiley.

Hofmann, S.G., Sawyer, A.T., Witt, A.A. and Oh, D. (2010) 'The effect of mindfulness-based therapy on anxiety and depression: A meta-analytic review', *Journal of Consulting and Clinical Psychology* 78: 169–183.

Hölzel, B.K., Carmody, B., Vangel, M., Congleton, C., Yeramsetti, S.E., Gard, T. and Lazar, S.W. (2011a) 'Mindfulness practice leads to increases in regional brain gray matter density', *Psychiatry Research: Neuroimaging* 191: 36–43.

Hölzel, B.K., Lazar, S.W., Gard, T., Schuman-Olivier, Z., Vago, D.R. and Ott, U. (2011b) 'How does mindfulness meditation work? Proposing mechanisms of action from a conceptual and neural perspective', *Perspectives in Psychological Science* 6: 537–559.

Ilg, R., Wohlschläger, A.M., Gaser, C., Liebau, Y., Dauner, R., Wöller, A., et al. (2008) 'Gray matter increase induced by practice correlates with task-specific activation: A combined functional and morphometric magnetic resonance imaging study', *Journal of Neuroscience* 28: 4210–4215.

Jackson, F. (1982) 'Epiphenomenal qualia', *Philosophical Quarterly* 32: 127–136.

Jacobs, T.L., Shaver, P.R., Epel, E.S., Zanesco, A.P., Aichele, S.A., Bridwell, P.R. et al. (2011) 'Intensive meditation training, immune cell telomerase activity, and psychological mediators', *Psychoneuroendocrinology* 36, 5: 664–681.

Jamgon Mipham (2009) *Luminous Essence: A Guide to the Guhyagarbha Tantra,* Ithaca, NY: Snow Lion.

Jensen, C.G., Vangkilde, S., Frokjaer, V. and Hasselbalch, S.G. (2012) 'Mindfulness training affects attention – or is it attentional effort?' *Journal of Experimental Psychology: General* 141, 1: 106–123.

Jha, A.P., Krompinger, J. and Baime, M.J. (2007) 'Mindfulness training modifies subsystems of attention', *Cognitive, Affective and Behavioral Neuroscience* 7: 109–119.

Johnson, S.C., Baxter, L.C., Wilder, L.S., Pipe, J.G., Heiserman, J.E. and Prigatano, G.P. (2002) 'Neural correlates of self-reflection', *Brain* 125, 8: 1808–1814.

Kabat-Zinn, J. (1990) *Full Catastrophe of Living*, New York, NY: Delacorte Press.

Kabat-Zinn, J. (2003) 'Mindfulness-based interventions in context: past, present, and future', *Clinical Psychology: Science and Practice* 10: 144–156.

Kastenbaum, R. and Normand, C. (1990) 'Deathbed scenes as imagined by the young and experienced by the old', *Death Studies* 14: 201–217.

Kensinger, E.A. and Schacter, D.L. (2006) 'Processing emotional pictures and words: Effects of valence and arousal', *Cognitive, Affective and Behavioral Neuroscience* 6, 2: 110–126.

Khenpo Tsultrim Lodu (2006) *Teachings of Khenpo Tsulrim Lodu.* Beijing: Beijing Human Publications. (Tibetan: Pal Larungi Khenpo Tsultrim Lodu kyi sung bum zhug so.)

Koltko-Rivera, M.E. (2006) 'Rediscovering the later version of Maslow's hierarchy of needs: self-transcendence and opportunities for theory, research, and unification', *Review of General Psychology* 10, 4: 302–317.

Kozhevnikov, M., Louchakova, O., Josipovic, Z. and Motes, M.A. (2009) 'The enhancement of visuospatial processing efficiency through Buddhist deity meditation', *Psychological Science* 20: 645–653.

Kringelbach, M.L. and Berridge, K.C. (2009) 'Towards a functional neuro-anatomy of pleasure and happiness', *Trends in Cognitive Sciences* 13: 479–487.

LaBerge, S. (2002) 'Lucid dreaming: evidence and methodology', *Behavioral and Brain Sciences* 23, 6: 962–964.

Lambie, J.A. and Marcel, A.J. (2002) 'Consciousness and the varieties of emotion experience: a theoretical framework', *Psychological Review* 109, 2: 219–259.

Lampert, R., Shusterman, V., Burg, M., McPherson, C., Batsford, W., Goldberg, A. and Soufer, R. (2009) 'Anger-induced T-wave alternans predicts future ventricular arrhythmias in patients with implantable cardioverter-defibrillators', *Journal of American College of Cardiology* 53: 774–778.

Lane, R.D. (2000) 'Neural correlates of conscious emotional experience', in R.D. Lane, L. Nadel, G.L. Ahern, J.J.B. Allen, A.W. Kas8zniak, S.Z. Rapcsak and G.E. Schwartz (eds.) *Cognitive Neuroscience of Emotion* (pp. 345–370), New York, NY: Oxford University Press.

Lazar, S.W., Kerr, C.E., Wasserman, R.H., Gray, J.R., Greve, D.N., Treadway, M.T.et al. (2005) 'Meditation experience is associated with increased cortical thickness', *Neuroreport* 16, 17: 1893–1897.

Longchenpa (2011) *The Guhyagarbha Tantra*, trans. Lama Chonam and Sangye Khandro, Ithaca, NY: Snow Lion.

Lutz, A., Greischar, L.L., Rawlings, N.B., Ricard, M. and Davidson, R.J. (2004) 'Long-term meditators self-induce high-amplitude gamma synchrony during mental practice', *Proceedings of the National Academy of Sciences* 101: 16369–16373.

Lutz, A., Dunne, J.P. and Davidson, R.J. (2007) 'Meditation and the neuroscience of consciousness: an introduction', in P. D. Zelazo, M. Moscovitch and E. Thompson (eds.) *Cambridge Handbook of Consciousness*, New York, NY: Cambridge University Press.

Lutz, A., Slagter, H.A., Dunne, J.D. and Davidson, R.J. (2008a) ,Attention regulation and monitoring in meditation', *Trends in Cognitive Sciences* 12: 163–169.

Lutz A., Brefczynski-Lewis J., Johnstone T. and Davidson R.J. (2008b) 'Regulation of the neural circuitry of emotion by compassion meditation: effects of meditative expertise', *PLoS ONE* 3(3): e1897.

Lutz, A. Slagter, H.A., Rawlings, N.B., Francis, A.D., Greischar, L.L. and Davidson, R.J. (2009) ,Mental training enhances attentional stability: Neural and behavioral evidence', *Journal of Neuroscience* 29: 13418–13427.

MacLean, K.A., Ferrer, E., Aichele, S.R., Bridwell, D.A., Zanesco, A.P., Jacobs, T.L. et al. (2010) 'Intensive meditation training improves perceptual discrimination and sustained attention', *Psychological Science* 21, 6: 829–839.

Maslow, A.H. (1943) 'A theory of human motivation', *Psychological Review* 50: 370–396.

Matthews, E.E. and Cook, P.F. (2009) 'Relationships among optimism, well-being, self-transcendence, coping, and social support in women during treatment for breast cancer', *Psycho-Oncology* 18: 716–726.

Mipham Rinpoche, J. (1997) *Gateway to Knowledge,* Vol. 1., trans. E. P. Kunsang, Boudhanath, Hong Kong and Esby: Rangjung Yeshe Publications.

Mitchell, D.W. (2002) *Buddhism: Introducing the Buddhist experience,* New York: Oxford University Press.

Nagel, T. (1974) 'What is it like to be a bat?', *Philosophical Review* 4: 435–450.

Neff, K.D. (2003) 'Self-compassion: An alternative conceptualization of a healthy attitude toward oneself', *Self and Identity* 2: 85–102.

Neff, K.D. and Germer, C.K. (2013) 'A pilot study and randomized controlled trial of the mindful self-compassion program', *Journal of Clinical Psychology* 69: 28–44.

Neihart, M. (1999) 'The impact of giftedness on psychological well-being: What does the empirical literature say?', *Roeper Review* 22: 10–17.

Nielsen, L. and Kaszniak, A.W. (2007) 'Conceptual, theoretical, and methodological issues in inferring subjective emotional experience: Recommendations for researchers', in J.J.B. Allen and J. Coan (eds.) *The Handbook of Emotion Elicitation and Assessment* (pp. 361–375), New York: Oxford University Press.

Nyklíček, I. and Kuijpers, K.F. (2008) 'Effects of mindfulness-based stress reduction intervention on psychological well-being and quality of life: is increased mindfulness indeed the mechanism?', *Annals of Behavioral Medicine* 35: 331–340.

Olendzki, A. (2008) 'The real practice of mindfulness', *Buddhadharma: The Practitioner's Quarterly* Retrieved December 11, 2009 from http://www.the buddhadharma.com/issues/2008/fall/mindfulness.php.

Padmasambhava (1998) *Natural Liberation*, Boston, MA: Wisdom Publications.

Padmasambhava (1999) *Dakini Teachings: A Collection of Padmasambhava's Advice to the Dakini Yeshe Tsogyal,* Hong Kong: Rangjung Yeshe Publications.

Patrul Rinpoche (1998) *The Words of My Perfect Teacher*, Boston, MA: Shambhala.

Pedersen, S.S. and Denollet, J. (2003) 'Type D personality, cardiac events, and impaired quality of life: a review', *European Journal of Cardiovascular Prevention and Rehabilitation* 10: 241–248.

Petersen S.E., Posner M.I. (2012) 'The attention system of the human brain: 20 years after', *Annual Review of Neuroscience* 35: 73–89. Petersen, S.E. Van Mier, H., Fiez, J.A. and Raichle, M.E. (1998) 'The effects of practice on the functional anatomy of task performance', *Proceedings of the National Academy of Sciences* 95, 3: 853–860.

Popper, K.R. and Eccles, J.C. (1977) *The Self and its Brain*, Berlin: Springer-Verlag.

Powers, J. (1995) *Tibetan Buddhism*, Ithaca, NY: Snow Lion.

Rabjam, L. (1998) *Precious Treasury of the Way of Abiding (Seven Treasuries Series)*, transl. R. Barron, Junction City, CA: Padma Publishing.

Rabjam, L. (2010) *Natural Perfection: Lonchenpa's Radical Dzogchen*, Boston, MA: Wisdom Publications.

Raichle, M.E., MacLeod, A.M., Snyder, A.Z., Powers, W.J., Gusnard, D.A. and Shulman, G.L. (2001) 'A default mode of brain function', *Proceedings of the National Academy of Sciences* 98: 676–682.

Ricard, M. (2003) 'A Buddhist psychology', in Goleman, D. (ed.) *Destructive Emotions: A Scientific Dialogue with the Dalai Lama*, New York: Bantam Books.

Ridderinkhof, K.R., van den Wildenberg, W.P.M., Segalowitz, S.J. and Carter, C.S. (2004) 'Neurocognitive mechanisms of cognitive control: The role of prefrontal cortex in action selection, response inhibition, performance monitoring, and reward-based learning', *Brain and Cognition* 56: 129–140.

Roemer, L., Lee, J.K., Salters-Pedneault, K., Erisman, S.M., Orsillo, S.M. and Mennin, D.S. (2009) 'Mindfulness and emotion regulation difficulties in generalized anxiety disorder: Preliminary evidence for independent and overlapping contributions', *Behavior Therapy* 40, 2: 142–154.

Rosch, E. (2007) 'More than mindfulness: When you have a tiger by the tail, let it eat you', *Psychological Inquiry* 18: 258–264.

Ryff, C.D. and Singer, B.H. (2008) 'Know thyself and become what you are: a eudaimonic approach to psychological well-being', *Happiness Studies* 9: 13–39.

Santideva (1997) *A Guide to the Bodhisattva Way of Life*, transl. V.A. Wallace and B.A. Wallace, Ithaca, NY: Snow Lion.

Scherer, K.R. (1984) 'On the nature and function of emotion: A component process approach', in K.R. Scherer and P.E. Ekman (eds.) *Approaches to Emotion* (pp. 293–317), Hillsdale, NJ: Erlbaum.

Scherer, K.R. (2000) 'Psychological models of emotion', in J.C. Borod (ed.) *The Neuropsychology of Emotion* (pp. 137–162), New York, NY: Oxford University Press.

Scherer, K.R. (2003) 'Introduction: Cognitive components of emotion', in R.J. Davidson, K.R. Scherer and H.H. Goldsmith (eds.) *Handbook of Affective Sciences* (pp. 563–571), New York, NY: Oxford University Press.

Schooler, J.W. (2002) 'Re-representing consciousness: Dissociations between experience and meta-consciousness', *Trends in Cognitive Science* 6: 339–344.

Shapiro, D.H. (1992) 'A preliminary study of long term meditators: Goals, effects, religious orientation, cognitions', *Journal of Transpersonal Psychology* 24, 1: 23–39.

Shapiro, S.L., Carlson, L.E., Astin, J.A. and Freedman, B. (2006) 'Mechanisms of mindfulness', *Journal of Clinical Psychology* 62: 373–386.

Shapiro, S.L., Brown, K.W. and Biegel, G. (2007) 'Teaching self-care to caregivers: The effects of Mindfulness-Based Stress Reduction on the mental health of therapists in training', *Training and Education in Professional Psychology* 1: 105–115.

Shapiro, S.L., Oman, D., Thoresen, C.E., Plante, T.G. and Flinders, T. (2008) 'Cultivating mindfulness: effects on well-being', *Journal of Clinical Psychology* 64: 840–862.

Siegel, R.D., Germer, C.K. and Olendzki, A. (2008) 'Mindfulness: What is it? Where did it come from?', in F. Didonna (ed.) *Clinical Handbook of Mindfulness*, New York, NY: Springer.

Slagter, H.A., Lutz, A., Breischar, L., Francis, A.D., Nieuwenhuis, S., Davis, J.M. and Davidson, R.J. (2007) 'Mental training affects distribution of limited brain resources', *PLoS Biology* 5: 1228-1235.

Slotnick, S.D., Thompson, W.L. and Kosslyn, S.M. (2012) 'Visual memory and visual mental imagery recruit common control and sensory regions of the brain', *Cognitive Neuroscience* 3, 1: 14–20.

Smith, T.W., Glazer, K., Ruiz, J.M. and Gallo, L.C. (2004) 'Hostility, anger, aggressiveness, and coronary heart disease: an interpersonal perspective on personality, emotion, and health', *Journal of Personality* 72: 1217–1270.

Stapp, H.P. (1996) 'The hard problem: A quantum approach', *Journal of Consciousness Studies* 3, 3: 194–210.

Teasdale, J.D., Segal, Z. and Williams, J.M. (1995) 'How does cognitive therapy prevent depressive relapse and why should attentional control (mindfulness) training help?', *Behaviour Research and Therapy 33*, 1: 25–39.

Teasdale, J.D., Segal, Z.V., Williams, J.M.G., Ridgeway, V.A., Soulsby, J.M. and Lau, M.A. (2000) 'Prevention of relapse/recurrence in major depression by mindfulness-based cognitive therapy', *Journal of Consulting and Clinical Psychology* 68: 615–623.

Teasdale, J.D., Moore, R.G., Mayhurst, H., Pope, M., Williams, S. and Segal, Z.V. (2002) 'Metacognitive awareness and prevention of relapse in depression', *Journal of Consulting and Clinical Psychology* 70: 275–287.

Thera, N. (1962) *The Heart of Buddhist Meditation: A Handbook of Mental Training Based on the Buddha's Way of Mindfulness*, London: Rider.

Thera, N. (1998) *Abhidhamma Studies: Buddhist Explorations of Consciousness and Time* 4th edn, Boston, MA: Wisdom Publications.

Titchener, E.B. (1912) 'The schema of introspection', *American Journal of Psychology* 23: 485–508.

UNICEF. (2007) 'Child poverty in perspective: An overview of child wellbeing in rich countries. A comprehensive assessment of the lives and wellbeing of children and adolescents in the economically advanced nations', *Innocenti Report Card 7* UNICEF Innocenti Research Centre, Florence.

Urgesi C., Aglioti S. M., Skrap M. and Fabbro F. (2010) 'The spiritual brain: selective cortical lesions modulate human self-transcendence', *Neuron* 65: 309–319.

US Census Bureau (2005) Population Estimates by Demographic Characteristics. Table 2: Annual Estimates of the Population by Selected Age Groups and Sex for the United States: April 1, 2000 to July 1, 2004 (NC-EST2004-02) Source: Population Division, U.S. Census Bureau Release Date: June 9, 2005. http://www.census.gov/popest/national/asrh/.

Vanhaudenhuyse A et al. (2010) 'Default network connectivity reflects the level of consciousness in non-communicative brain-damaged patients', *Brain* 133: 161–171.

Varela, F.J. (1997) *Sleeping, Dreaming, and Dying*, Boston, MA: Wisdom Publications.

Varela, F.J., Thompson, E. and Rosch, E. (1991) *The Embodied Mind*, Cambridge, MA: MIT Press.

Wallace, B.A. (1999a) 'The Buddhist tradition of Samatha: Methods for refining and examining consciousness', *Journal of Consciousness Studies* 6: 175–187.

Wallace, B.A. (1999b) *The Four Immeasurables: Cultivating a Boundless Heart*, Ithaca, NY: Snow Lion Publications.

Wallace, B.A. (2006) *The Attention Revolution: Unlocking the Power of the Focused Mind,* Somerville, MA: Wisdom Publications.

Wallace, A.B. (2007) *Contemplative Science: Where Buddhism and Neuroscience Converge*, New York, NY: Columbia University Press.

Wallace B.A. and Shapiro S.L. (2006) 'Mental balance and well-being: Building bridges between Buddhism and Western psychology', *American Psychologist* 61: 690–701.

Watson, J.B. (1913) 'Psychology as the behaviorist views it', *Psychological Review* 20, 2: 158-177.

Weisberg D.S., Keil F.C., Goodstein J., Rawson E. and Gray, J.R. (2008) 'The seductive allure of neuroscience explanations', *Journal of Cognitive Neuroscience* 20: 470–477.

Winkielman, P. and Berridge, K.C. (2004) 'Unconscious emotion', *Current Directions in Psychological Science* 13: 120–123.

Index